T0205977

Lecture Notes in Computer Science 12332

More information about this series at http://www.springer.com/series/7410

Awais Rashid · Peter Popov (Eds.)

Critical Information Infrastructures Security

15th International Conference, CRITIS 2020
Bristol, UK, September 2–3, 2020
Proceedings

 Springer

Editors
Awais Rashid (ID)
Department of Computer Science
University of Bristol
Bristol, UK

Peter Popov (ID)
Department of Computer Science
City, University of London
London, UK

ISSN 0302-9743   ISSN 1611-3349 (electronic)
Lecture Notes in Computer Science
ISBN 978-3-030-58294-4   ISBN 978-3-030-58295-1 (eBook)
https://doi.org/10.1007/978-3-030-58295-1

LNCS Sublibrary: SL4 – Security and Cryptology

This Springer imprint is published by the registered company Springer Nature Switzerland AG
The registered company address is: Gewerbestrasse 11, 6330 Cham, Switzerland

Preface

This volume contains the proceedings of the 15th International Conference on Critical Information Infrastructures Security (CRITIS 2020). The conference was organized by the Bristol Cyber Security Group at University of Bristol and held for the first time in the UK during September 2–3, 2020.

CRITIS 2020 continued the well-established series of successful CRITIS conferences and yet was somewhat different from the previous editions. Due to the COVID-19 pandemic, and in order to ensure safety of participants, the conference was conducted as an online event.

The conference was addressed by three keynote speakers:

- Dr. Alvaro A. Cardenas, University of California, Santa Cruz, USA
- Prof. Chris Hankin, Imperial College London, UK
- Prof. Dimitris Gritzalis, Athens University of Economics and Business, Greece

This year's edition of CRITIS offered three strands of contributions:

- Regular technical papers
- Short two-page industrial/practical experience papers
- Short two-page reports on testbeds and datasets

Due to the extraordinary circumstances this year due to the COVID-19 pandemic, the number of submissions to the conference was lower than in the previous years.

- 17 regular papers were received. All papers in this category were reviewed by either four or five reviewers independently followed by a discussion among the reviewers and reaching a consensus on the submissions. Five full papers, i.e. the acceptance rate was just under 30%, thus maintaining the quality of the conference. One paper was accepted as a short paper to ensure that the ideas presented were disseminated to the community.
- Two industrial/practical experience papers were received and both were accepted. These submissions were reviewed by the program co-chairs independently followed by a discussion. These papers were not included in the proceedings but are available on the CRITIS 2020 website.
- One paper was invited as a testbed report and is also available on the CRITIS 2020 website.
- The program also featured a tour and demonstration of the Bristol Cyber Security Group testbed on cyber security of critical national infrastructure.

The co-chairs of the International Program Committee (IPC) are grateful to the members of the IPC for the effort they have put into their reviews and the subsequent discussions, which allowed us to maintain the quality of the conference.

The accepted papers are grouped in the following categories:

- Invited papers
- Attacks and vulnerabilities
- Threat modeling and monitoring
- Networks and IoT

The papers appear in these proceedings under the same categories.

CRITIS 2020 will be remembered for a number of reasons: as a difficult year for the entire CRITIS community due to the COVID-19 pandemic; for the lack of socializing at the conference, which has always been an essential part of building the CRITIS community; and for the missed opportunity for non-UK colleagues to explore the great and vibrant city of Bristol and its proud history.

As organizers of this year's CRITIS, we are pleased and proud that despite the significant challenges we had to face, CRITIS not merely survived, but will be remembered for a good technical program with interesting technical contributions and invited talks.

We would also like to thank all members of the Organizing Committee at the University of Bristol, especially Dr. Louise Evans and Dr. Ben Shreeve, who helped with the preparation and smooth (remote) running of the conference.

September 2020   Awais Rashid
                                                                  Peter Popov

Organization

Organizing Committee

General Chair

Awais Rashid   University of Bristol, UK

Program Co-chairs

Awais Rashid   University of Bristol, UK
Peter Popov   City, University of London, UK

Local Organising Chair

Barney Craggs   University of Bristol, UK

Publicity Chair

Nils Ole Tippenhauer   CISPA Helmholtz Center for Information Security, Germany

Conference Manager

Louise Evans   University of Bristol, UK

Proceedings and Platform Support

Benjamin Shreeve   University of Bristol, UK

Technical Program Committee

Peter Popov (Chair)	City, University of London, UK
Awais Rashid (Chair)	University of Bristol, UK
Cristina Alcaraz	University of Malaga, Spain
Magnus Almgren	Chalmers University of Technology, Sweden
Fabrizio Baiardi	University of Pisa, Italy
Sandro Bologna	AIIC, Italy
Alvaro Cardenas	The University of Texas at Dallas, USA
Tom Chothia	University of Birmingham, UK
Gregorio D'Agostino	ENEA, Italy
Geert Deconinck	KU Leuven, Belgium
Dimitris Gritzalis	Athens University of Economics and Business, Greece
Bernhard Hämmerli	Acris GmbH, Switzerland
Chris Hankin	Imperial College London, UK
Grigore M. Havarneanu	International Union of Railways (UIC), France
Mikel Iturbe	Mondragon University, Spain

Zbigniew Kalbarczyk	University of Illinois at Urbana-Champaign, USA
Sokratis Katsikas	Open University of Cyprus, Cyprus
Marieke Klaver	TNO, The Netherlands
Vytis Kopustinskas	European Commission, Italy
Panayiotis Kotzanikolaou	University of Piraeus, Greece
Marina Krotofil	Hamburg University of Technology, Germany
Javier Lopez	University of Malaga, Spain
Linas Martišauskas	Lithuanian Energy Institute, Lithuania
Marcelo Masera	European Commission, Belgium
Kieran Mclaughlin	Queen's University Belfast, UK
Alain Mermoud	Cyber-Defence Campus, Switzerland
Simin Nadjm-Tehrani	Linköping University, Sweden
Stefano Panzieri	Roma Tre University, Italy
Ludovic Pietre-Cambacedes	EDF, France
Anne Remke	University of Münster, Germany
Kizito Salako	City, University London, UK
Henrik Sandberg	KTH Royal Institute of Technology, Sweden
Roberto Setola	Università Campus Bio-Medico di Roma, Italy
Vladimir Stankovic	City, University London, UK
Nils Ole Tippenhauer	CISPA Helmholtz Center for Information Security, Germany
Alberto Tofani	ENEA, Italy
Claire Vishik	Intel Corporation, UK
Jianying Zhou	Singapore University of Technology and Design, Singapore
Inga Žutautaitė	Lithuanian Energy Institute, Lithuania

CRITIS Steering Committee

Chairs

Bernhard M. Hämmerli	Acris GmbH, Switzerland
Javier Lopez	University of Malaga, Spain
Stephen D. Wolthusen	Royal Holloway, University of London, UK, and NTNU, Norway

Members

Robin Bloomfield	City, University London, UK
Sandro Bologna	AIIC, Italy
Gregorio D'Agostino	ENEA, Italy
Grigore Havarneanu	International Union of Railways (UIC), France
Sokratis K. Katsikas	Open University of Cyprus, Cyprus
Elias Kyriakides	University of Cyprus, Cyprus
Eric Luiijf	TNO (retired), The Netherlands
Marios M. Polycarpou	University of Cyprus, Cyprus
Reinhard Posch	Technical University Graz, Austria

Erich Rome	Fraunhofer IAIS, Germany
Antonio Scala	IMT-CNR, Italy
Inga Šarūnienė	Lithuanian Energy Institute, Lithuania
Roberto Setola	Università Campus Bio-Medico di Roma, Italy
Nils Kalstad Svendsen	Gjovik University College, Norway
Marianthi Theocharidou	European Commission, Italy

Contents

Invited Paper

Trustworthy Inter-connected Cyber-Physical Systems

Chris Hankin$^{(\boxtimes)}$ ⬤ and Martín Barrère ⬤

Institute for Security Science and Technology, Imperial College London, London, UK
{c.hankin,m.barrere}@imperial.ac.uk
https://www.imperial.ac.uk/people/c.hankin,
https://www.imperial.ac.uk/people/m.barrere

Abstract. In this paper we identify some of the particular challenges that are encountered when trying to secure cyber-physical systems. We describe three of our current activities: the architecture of a system for monitoring cyber-physical systems; a new approach to modelling dependencies in such systems which leads to a measurement of the security of the system – interpreted as the least effort that an attacker has to expend to compromise the operation; and an approach to optimising the diversity of products used in a system with a view to slowing the propagation of malware. We conclude by discussing how these different threads of work contribute to meeting the challenges and identify possible avenues for future development, as well as providing some pointers to other work.

Keywords: Cyber-physical systems · Cyber security · Critical infrastructure

1 Introduction

There are various estimates of the numbers of devices connected to the Internet but it is likely to be about 30 billion this year with a few thousand additional IoT devices being added every minute. Some companies estimate that there will be a few hundred billion by 2030. Given that each of us can only manage a small number of IT devices, it is inevitable that many of those devices will be deployed in cyber-physical systems (CPS) – domestic heating, lighting and environmental controls, manufacturing processes and critical infrastructures. The rapid pace of digitalisation of these functions and services will pose many new opportunities but also new threats. One source of the new threats is the increasing inter-connectedness of such systems and a greater reliance on computers and communications which in turn rely on a resilient power distribution network. The rapid growth of numbers of inter-connected devices has out-stripped the ability of legislators to keep up; safety is a major attribute of many cyber-physical systems and it is imperative that these systems can be shown to be trustworthy.

Partially supported by EPSRC award EP/R022844/1 (RITICS) and EU Horizon 2020 grant 739551 (KIOS Centre of Excellence).

A. Rashid and P. Popov (Eds.): CRITIS 2020, LNCS 12332, pp. 3–13, 2020.
https://doi.org/10.1007/978-3-030-58295-1_1

Trustworthy, inter-connected cyber-physical systems are the focus of RIT-ICS, the UK <u>R</u>esearch <u>I</u>nstitute in <u>T</u>rustworthy <u>I</u>nter-connected <u>C</u>yber-physical <u>S</u>ystems[1]. The institute is addressing the following key questions:

Q1. Do we understand the harm that cyber threats pose to the provision of critical systems?

Q2. Can we confidently articulate these threats as risk to delivery of critical systems at a business and national level?

Q3. Are there novel effective and efficient interventions for businesses or governments to reduce the risks to critical systems?

Q4. How can we best understand and compare both the effectiveness and costs of potential interventions? These might include technical interventions such as altering system architecture, through to policy interventions by governments and regulators.

Q5. How can we best detect intrusion in critical systems, including embedded and bespoke systems, and how should incident response differ to established practices for enterprise IT? The network traffic in an Industrial Control System (ICS) network is much more predictable than in the Internet, so Intrusion Detection Systems (IDS) can be very effective. Intrusion Prevention Systems (IPS) block unexpected traffic and could be considered to be more risky in an ICS environment – potentially blocking important emergency traffic.

Q6. What are the obstacles to (perceived) best practice being applied to critical systems?

There are many aspects to trustworthiness and our main focus is on cyber security – the system should be protected from interference by malicious attackers. Other aspects include safety, reliability and correctness – where the latter is tested against some formally specified requirements. These different dimensions are clearly inter-related since it is unlikely that an insecure system could be safe

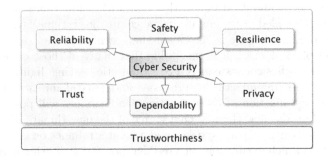

Fig. 1. The role of cyber security for trustworthy inter-connected cyber-physical systems

---

[1] See https://ritics.org.

or reliable[2]. As illustrated in Fig. 1, our vision is that trustworthiness builds upon a number of fundamental disciplines where cyber security plays a vital role and has an impact on all of them.

2   Challenges

There are a number of obstacles and challenges to achieving trustworthiness which include:

C1. Many cyber security specialists start their training as computer scientists and this often leaves them poorly equipped to reason about physical phenomena. It also raises the issue that good solutions for the cyber security of IT systems are not always appropriate for CPS.

C2. Inter-connectedness leads to complex inter-dependencies which are difficult to identify and reason about. There may be a problem of undesirable emergent behaviour arising at the interfaces between different systems.

C3. Digitalisation has led to a tendency for homogeneity – the same technical solution (software, hardware and middleware) being used across disparate systems. This is one of many factors, alongside legacy systems and unpatched software, that facilitates the migration of worm malware as seen with the rapid spread of the WannaCry ransomware.

C4. The increasing reliance on Artificial Intelligence solutions – particularly Machine Learning – which are difficult to reason about.

In the US, infrastructure security falls within the remit of the Cybersecurity and Infrastructure Security Agency (CISA)[3] which is part of the Department of Homeland Security. CISA has identified a number of emerging trends that impact on the security of ICS; in addition to some of the challenges identified by RITICS they include:

– Bring Your Own Device (BYOD) – possibly surprising but some vendors have used the possibility of BYOD to access control systems, particularly in an Industrial Internet of Things setting, as a major selling point.
– Virtual Machine Technologies – which is often seen as a way of reducing capital equipment costs by, for example, hosting the Demilitarised Zone and the ICS servers on the same physical machine.
– ICS Supply Chain Management – many suppliers of equipment and software for critical infrastructure source components from around the world. Major systems, such as aircraft, may rely on thousands of suppliers. Managing such an ecosystem and ensuring the security of the end product is becoming a major challenge.

---

[2] This is debatable; for example, whilst a cryptographic algorithm may be insecure, it might require so much computational resource to break that it is still safe to use it – although emerging technologies such as quantum computation may change this argument.

[3] https://www.cisa.gov/national-cybersecurity-communications-integration-center.

– Leveraging Cloud Services in ICS – some researchers and organisations are
  beginning to consider how cloud services may be used for data storage and
  to provide other services to support their ICS architectures.

3   Our Approach

We are working in a number of areas which address some of these challenges and
we highlight three pieces of work in this section.

3.1   Real-Time CPS Monitoring for Security Research

Monitoring systems are essential to understand and control the behaviour of systems and networks. CPS are particularly delicate under that perspective since
they involve real-time constraints and physical phenomena that are not usually
considered in common IT solutions. Unfortunately, the security research community lacks open and configurable monitoring tools that can be adapted to
different CPS research scenarios and consider real-time aspects as well. Therefore, there is a need for publicly available monitoring tools able to contemplate
these aspects. We have developed an approach, called CPS-MT [1], which is a
proof-of-concept of a versatile, real-time CPS monitoring tool, with a particular
focus on security research.

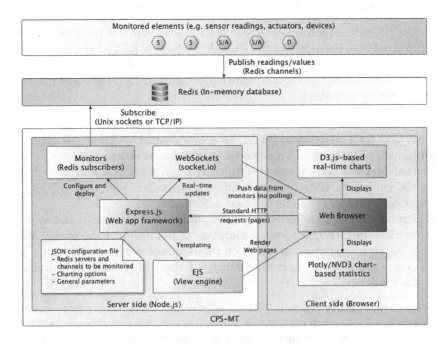

Fig. 2. CPS-MT high level architecture

Our monitoring approach relies on the architecture illustrated in Fig. 2. The upper layer represents the CPS elements to be monitored, e.g., readings from PLCs, actuators, sensor readings, etc. The middle layer acts as a broker between the elements being monitored and CPS-MT. We use Redis [2] to implement this layer. Redis is a fast in-memory database that stores data in the form of key-value pairs. The main idea is that monitored elements publish their data via Redis channels and CPS-MT subscribes to these predefined channels in order to receive updates in real time. This makes CPS-MT almost agnostic to what is being monitored, and thus very flexible. Since our main focus is on security research, we assume that cyber attacks conducted within the framework will not target Redis but rather the CPS components within the experimental setup. This is because the role of Redis it to record the data during an attack (e.g. what data PLCs and sensors send, what PLCs receive, etc.) for posterior analysis and research. The bottom layer illustrates the main components of the CPS-MT client-server architecture. The main goal of the server is to monitor the activity on Redis channels and report updates to the client side. The client (Web browser) will display and/or capture this new data as it becomes available. We use WebSockets to implement a two-way communication between the server and the client [3]. This allows the server to push data directly into the client

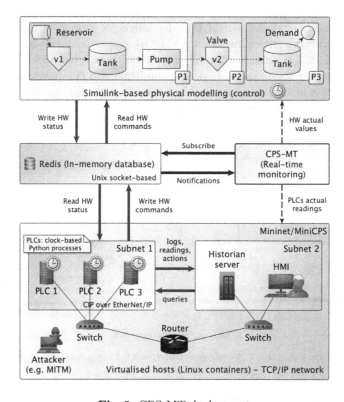

Fig. 3. CPS-MT deployment

in real time. WebSockets eliminate long polling and multiple client requests as happens with traditional HTTP-based approaches. Visualisation aspects are handled by the client side and rely mostly on JavaScript and D3.js [4]. The system also allows the exploration of captured sessions in order to analyse CPS behaviour over specific periods of time.

We have used CPS-MT to analyse the behaviour and impact of MITM attacks over a simulated water treatment plant built with MiniCPS [5]. Figure 3 shows the details of the CPS-MT deployment within this scenario. MiniCPS is an extensible Python-based simulation framework built on top of Mininet [6], which implements simulated CPS components such as PLCs, their interactions with physical devices, and standard industrial protocols such as Modbus/TCP and CIP over Ethernet/IP. We have extended MiniCPS to also support Redis as its data store, thus enabling CPS-MT to monitor the status of the whole simulation process, including cyber attacks.

3.2 Measuring Cyber-Physical Security

Over the last years, ICS have become increasingly exposed to a wide range of cyber-physical threats. Efficient models and techniques able to capture their complex structure and identify critical cyber-physical components are therefore essential. AND/OR graphs have proven very useful in this context as they are able to represent intricate logical interdependencies among ICS components. However, identifying critical nodes in AND/OR graphs is an NP-complete problem. In addition, ICS settings normally involve various cyber and physical security measures that simultaneously protect multiple ICS components in overlapping manners, which makes this problem even harder. For example, a number of sensors and actuators may be protected by a fenced area but some of them may be additionally secured in a locked enclosure. In [7] we have developed a

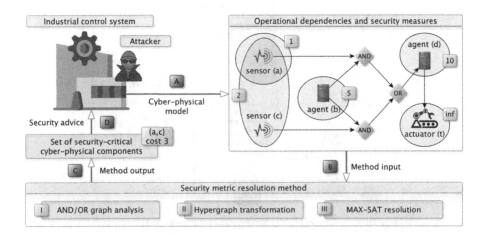

Fig. 4. Measuring ICS cyber-physical security via minimum-effort attack strategies

security metric based on weighted AND/OR hypergraphs which efficiently identifies the set of critical ICS components and security measures that should be compromised, with minimum cost (effort) for an attacker, in order to disrupt the operation of vital ICS assets. In particular, we use AND/OR hypergraphs to model dependencies between ICS components and the security measures used to protect them as shown in Fig. 4. We then transform this model into a weighted logical formulation that is used to solve a maximum satisfiability (MAX-SAT) problem. The solution to this problem indicates the minimum cost set of cyber-physical components and security measures that must be compromised to disrupt the operation of the system.

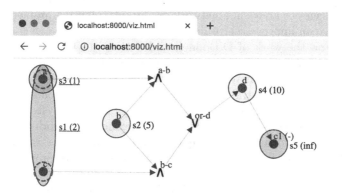

Fig. 5. The output from META4ICS for scenario in Fig. 4

We have developed an open source tool called META4ICS [8] that implements this methodology and outputs the computed metric in a JSON file that is later used to display the solution on a web browser. Figure 5 shows the output of META4ICS for the ICS scenario illustrated in Fig. 4 where the critical components $\{a, c\}$ are highlighted with red dashed circles and the critical security measures $\{s1, s3\}$ are underlined and highlighted in red. META4ICS uses a parallel SAT-solving architecture which increases its performance and allows it to scale to graphs with thousands of nodes in seconds. In particular, a significant part of our evaluation benchmark [9] has been included in the body of optimization problems used in the MaxSAT Evaluation 2019[4] to assess the participant MaxSAT solvers. Interestingly, none of the solvers evaluated in the competition performed better than the others on every instance of our dataset. The reason is that distinct MaxSAT solvers generally use very different resolution techniques. As a consequence, the outcome obtained from diversity (using parallel solving) is in fact quite good. Although further work is required, these results also indicate that our approach can be potentially used in dynamic scenarios to prioritise assets and security measures during ongoing intrusions and cyber attacks.

---

[4] https://maxsat-evaluations.github.io/2019/.

3.3 Software Diversity

It has been recognised since the 1970s that diversity in software can lead to increased reliability in embedded systems. Baudry and MonPerrus [10] provide an excellent survey of different approaches. The survey article distinguishes two main themes in diversity engineering: managed diversity; and automated diversity. A key technique in the former is n-version design or programming. Automated approaches include randomisation techniques and obfuscation.

One can consider diversity at different scales ranging from individual statements within a program through larger code fragments to the level of networks. Within the managed diversity strand, O'Donnell and Sethu [11] consider software diversity at the level of networks, they present the allocation of different software packages to nodes in a network as a graph colouring problem and show how diversity can improve the resilience of a network.

Building on the work of O'Donnell and Sethu, we [12] have developed an approach at the network level. In contrast to much of the earlier work, we model networks in which nodes may be running multiple, vulnerable products and in which there may be constraints on which products can cohabit a node – for example some products will not run on certain operating systems. The main objective of our work is to study the similarities between products which may cause malware to propagate more rapidly through a network – the output is an optimal allocation of products to nodes that slows malware propagation as far as possible.

We use a notion of similarity which is based on shared vulnerabilities; information about vulnerabilities can be extracted from the National Vulnerability Database (NVD) using tools such as CVE-SEARCH [13]. The similarity of two products is computed as the number of shared vulnerabilities divided by the total number of vulnerabilities of the two – this is called the Jaccard similarity coefficient. The Jaccard similarity coefficient is one way to quantify how similar a pair of software products are, giving a measure of how likely it is that they could be affected by the same malware. It is important to note that, even though we use a similarity measure based on shared vulnerabilities, other measures such as the amount of shared code base could be used instead. The underlying premise is that the more similar two products are, whatever the measure, the more likely it is that malware (even 0-days) will propagate between them. Our work allows multiple services, each of which can be realised by multiple products, to be assigned to each node; it also allows local and global constraints on the combination of products in a solution. The optimisation problem can be efficiently solved and results in an assignment of products to nodes.

We then measure the improved resilience of the diversified network in terms of a network diversity metric [14] and Mean-time-to-compromise (MTTC), to verify the effectiveness of our approach. We have shown the competitive scalability of our approach in finding optimal solutions within a couple of seconds to minutes for networks of large scale (up to 10,000 hosts) and high density (up to 240,000 edges).

Whilst it is true that the NVD concentrates on vulnerabilities in software that is typically deployed on traditional IT systems it is noteworthy that, for example, it contains nearly 200 vulnerabilities that relate to programmable logic controllers (PLCs) and that over 20% of these have been published since January 2019. It is to be expected that, as cyber physical systems become more prevalent, the rate of discovery of new vulnerabilities in devices and products developed for such systems will rapidly increase.

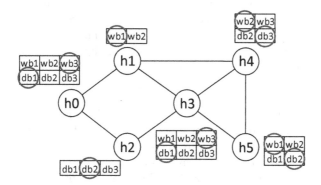

Fig. 6. One possible allocation

A simple example of the output of the work from [12] is shown in Fig. 6 – in this simple network, there is a choice between various web browsers and database systems at each node. The allocation is illustrated by the red circles. Currently, our approach optimises the allocation of network resources from a static perspective. However, it could be integrated with vulnerability management tools to support dynamic network reconfiguration as new vulnerabilities and security patches are disclosed. Moreover, the proposed technique could also be used to improve existing defence methods such as Moving Target Defence (MTD) and design diversity-based MTD methods to address dynamic scenarios.

4   Conclusions

We have presented our work which addresses some of the challenges identified in the opening sections of this short paper. In each case, the work has been supported by proof-of-concept implementations and, in the cited papers, we have demonstrated that the approaches scale appropriately.

Our work on monitoring provides an experimental framework that could be used to evaluate different approaches to intrusion detection and prevention. It also provides an experimental infrastructure which can be used to help cyber security professionals to gain a better understanding of CPS in line with challenge C1. In the long term, we envisage a hybrid infrastructure with hardware-in-the-loop and emulations of typical control systems components.

The work on measurement explicitly addresses the inter-dependencies inside a critical infrastructure. This is a first step and does not directly address the challenge C2 about emergent behaviour identified earlier. However, there is no a priori reason why our techniques could not be used to study inter-dependencies in Systems of Systems. This may require an enrichment of the logic used to represent dependencies beyond the simple propositional connectives used at present.

It is well-recognised that software/hardware diversity improves resilience of systems in the face of increasing digitalisation as stated in challenge C3. Our work represents an advance on the state-of-the-art in modelling multi-dimensional diversity in a network whereas previous work has been based on much simpler graph colouring. There is a cost associated with diversity, both in terms of training and higher operational costs (e.g. licensing, maintenance). We currently optimise for reducing the rate of malware propagation in a network but future work should take these socio-technical considerations into account. This could involve a game-theoretic approach, as used in [15], which can account for various types of cost. Others, for example Michael Franz [16], are actively working on practical and inexpensive approaches to software diversity.

Machine Learning algorithms are increasingly used in security applications for intrusion detection both in enterprise IT systems and, more recently in ICS. It is also now well-known that such algorithms are susceptible to attack by "poisoning" of training data or through techniques involving the introduction of perturbations in live data which are designed to be undetectable. This has led to a sub-discipline of adversarial machine learning. In [17,18] we examine the vulnerability of such intrusion detection systems to adversarial attacks. The attacker is able to manipulate the data sent to an IDS and seeks to hide their presence. This is proving to be a fruitful area of research. Our preliminary results are promising so far, although we plan to further extend our contributions and also consider fundamental aspects aligned with challenge C4 such as interpretability, transparency, and explainability for AI-based trustworthy cyber-physical systems.

Other partners in RITICS have been studying issues relating to supply chain security (particularly in the context of the EU Network and Information Security (NIS) Directive – see [19] for example), the interactions between various non-functional requirements in a CPS (notably safety and security) and the secure use of cloud services. Further details can be found on the RITICS website[5] and the KIOS Centre of Excellence (KIOS CoE)[6] which has partially funded and supported our work.

References

1. Barrère, M., Hankin, C., Barboni, A., Zizzo, G., Boem, F., Maffeis, S., Parisini, T.: CPS-MT: a real-time cyber-physical system monitoring tool for security research. In: 24th IEEE International Conference on Embedded and Real-Time Computing Systems and Applications, pp. 240–241. IEEE Computer Society (2018). https://doi.org/10.1109/RTCSA.2018.00040

---

[5] https://ritics.org.

[6] https://www.kios.ucy.ac.cy.

2. Redis. https://redis.io/. Accessed July 2020
3. RFC 6455 - The WebSocket Protocol. https://tools.ietf.org/html/rfc6455. Accessed July 2020
4. D3.js - Data Driven Documents. https://d3js.org/. Accessed July 2020
5. Antonioli, D., Tippenhauer, N.O.: MiniCPS: a toolkit for security research on CPS networks. In: Proceedings of the First ACM Workshop on Cyber-Physical Systems-Security and/or PrivaCy, CPS-SPC 2015 (2015)
6. Mininet. http://mininet.org/. Accessed July 2020
7. Barrère, M., Hankin, C., Nicolaou, N., Eliades, D.G., Parisini, T.: Measuring cyber-physical security in industrial control systems via minimum-effort attack strategies. J. Inf. Secur. Appl. **52** (2020). https://doi.org/10.1016/j.jisa.2020.102471
8. Barrère, M.: META4ICS - Metric Analyser for Industrial Control Systems, May 2019. https://github.com/mbarrere/meta4ics
9. Barrère, M., Hankin, C., Nicolaou, N., Eliades, D.G., Parisini, T.: MaxSAT evaluation 2019 - benchmark: identifying security-critical cyber-physical components in weighted AND/OR graphs. In: MaxSAT Evaluation 2019 (MSE 2019) (2019). https://arxiv.org/abs/1911.00516
10. Baudry, B., Monperrus, M.: The multiple facets of software diversity: recent developments in year 2000 and beyond. ACM Comput. Surv. **48**(1), 1–26 (2015)
11. O'Donnell, A.J., Sethu, H.: On achieving software diversity for improved network security using distributed coloring algorithms. In: Proceedings of the 11th ACM Conference on Computer and Communications Security, pp. 121–131. ACM, New York (2004)
12. Li, T., Feng, C., Hankin, C.: Improving ICS cyber resilience through optimal diversification of network resources. CoRR, abs/1811.00142 (2018). To appear at DSN 2020. http://arxiv.org/abs/1811.00142
13. Moreels, P.-J., Dulaunoy, A.: CVE-SEARCH, GitHub repository at https://github.com/cve-search/cve-search. Accessed 2020
14. Zhang, M., Wang, L., Jajodia, S., Singhal, A., Albanese, M.: Network diversity: a security metric for evaluating the resilience of networks against zero-day attacks. IEEE Trans. Inf. Forensics Secur. **11**(5), 1071–1086 (2016)
15. Fielder, A., Panaousis, E.A., Malacaria, P., Hankin, C., Smeraldi, F.: Decision support approaches for cyber security investment. Decis. Support Syst. **86**, 13–23 (2016). https://doi.org/10.1016/j.dss.2016.02.012
16. Franz, M.: Making multivariant programming practical and inexpensive. IEEE Secur. Priv. **16**, 90–94 (2018). https://doi.org/10.1109/MSP.2018.2701161
17. Zizzo, G., Hankin, C., Maffeis, S., Jones, K.: Adversarial machine learning beyond the image domain. In: Proceedings of the 56th Annual Design Automation Conference 2019, p. 176. ACM Press (2019). https://doi.org/10.1145/3316781.3323470
18. Zizzo, G., Hankin, C., Maffeis, S., Jones, K.: Intrusion detection for industrial control systems: evaluation analysis and adversarial attacks. CoRR, abs/1911.04278 (2019). http://arxiv.org/abs/1911.04278
19. Michalec, A., Van Der Linden, D., Milyaeva, S., Rashid, A.: Industry responses to the European directive on security of network and information systems (NIS): understanding policy implementation practices across critical infrastructures. https://research-information.bris.ac.uk/en/publications/industry-responses-to-the-european-directive-on-security-of-netwo. Accessed July 2020

Attacks and Vulnerabilities

A Tale of Two Testbeds: A Comparative Study of Attack Detection Techniques in CPS

Surabhi Athalye[(✉)], Chuadhry Mujeeb Ahmed, and Jianying Zhou

Singapore University of Technology and Design, Singapore, Singapore
{surabhi_athalye,mujeeb_chuadhry,jianying_zhou}@sutd.edu.sg

Abstract. Attack detection in cyber-physical systems (CPS) has been approached in several ways due to the complex interactions among the physical and cyber components. A comprehensive study is presented in this paper to compare different attack detection techniques and evaluate them based on a defined set of metrics. This work investigates model-based attack detectors that use mathematical system models with the sensor/actuator set as the input/output of the underlying physical processes. The detection mechanisms include statistical change monitoring (CUSUM and Bad-Data detectors) and a machine learning based-method that analyses the residual signal. This is a tale of two testbeds, a secure water treatment plant (SWaT) and a water distribution plant (WADI), which serve as case studies for the diverse range of CPS infrastructures found in cities today. The performance of the detection methods is experimentally studied by executing various types of attacks on the plants.

Keywords: Cyber-physical systems · Water treatment systems · Water distribution systems · Model-based attack detection

1 Introduction

A cyber-physical system (CPS) comprises of physical infrastructure that is controlled by computation and communication frameworks. It includes a combination of interconnected components such as Programmable Logic Controllers (PLCs), sensors, actuators, a Supervisory Control and Data Acquisition (SCADA) workstation, and a Human Machine Interface (HMI) that communicate across a network. The PLCs check the present state of the system through the SCADA and implement the corresponding control actions to facilitate the proper progress and functioning of the sub-processes.

The normal operation of a CPS requires the network and physical elements to work in tandem, for they directly influence the physical processes. Communication among such industrial IoTs is helpful but it also exposes them to malicious entities [1,2]. This makes the design of security measures for a CPS more complicated as compared to those meant for pure IT systems because attacks can occur in both the cyber and physical domain [3].

Since an inter-connected CPS also incorporates wireless communication, the infrastructure is prone to remote breaches and attacks [4]. This can be detrimental as it endangers the crucial communication links between the different nodes in a CPS, allowing

© Springer Nature Switzerland AG 2020
A. Rashid and P. Popov (Eds.): CRITIS 2020, LNCS 12332, pp. 17–30, 2020.
https://doi.org/10.1007/978-3-030-58295-1_2

them to be manipulated by external entities. By influencing the underlying processes in a CPS, cyber attacks could sabotage its physical infrastructure. Physical attacks can damage the sensors or other devices, which compromises the integrity of the data. This is a major risk as it results in faulty data being forwarded to the controllers, which adversely affects the control actions that are computed based on it. Conventionally, security research is focused on detecting anomalies in the communication network part of a CPS [5]. However, physical attacks can be more difficult to detect as they may not be reflected in the system network [6].

In this work, case studies are done on a water treatment testbed and a water distribution testbed, wherein model-based approaches for attack detection are considered. The sensor and control data from these plants under normal operation is used to derive Linear Time-Invariant (LTI) system models. These models are created using a control-theoretic approach, thus allowing the physical dynamics of the underlying processes to be captured analytically. The attack detection methods are then applied to the residual (the difference between the estimated and actual sensor values).

The detection performances of three attack detection techniques are evaluated in this paper. The first two methods are statistical change detectors called Cumulative Sum (CUSUM) and Bad-Data detectors that identify instances of abnormal data using empirically determined thresholds. The third technique is a machine learning-based device fingerprinting method called *NoisePrint* [3].

While gauging the performance, apart from precision, another important consideration for the attack detection techniques is their sensitivity. This refers to their tendency of raising false alarms when the plants operate normally. This is vital due to its implications in practical scenarios, wherein a system of numerous physical components needs to be checked. Hence, the detection mechanisms are evaluated under normal operating conditions as well as when the plants are under several attacks to acquire a comprehensive understanding of their performance.

The motivation for this work is to exhaustively test and compare attack detection techniques for CPS on different testbeds. The implementation of such methods on real-world systems is able to provide some useful insights to address the following issues:

1. *Impact of Noise on System Models*: The implementation and verification of theoretical models brought up some problems, one of them being the noise from the process for each different run. It can be seen that the effect of noise from the environmental disturbances on the process causes unpredictable deviations from its modelled behavior.
2. *Sensor Faults*: One of the problems was the unseen faults in sensors even during the normal operation of the plant, which hindered the creation of useful system models. This means that during the data collection under normal operation, the components must be thoroughly checked to ensure that all of them are functioning properly.
3. *Data Availability and Reliability*: Data availability plays a vital role in the design and performance of an anomaly detector. Prior to model creation, it is necessary to procure sufficient data that (a) represents the components' entire performance cycle, and (b) covers all possible modes of the operation of the Industrial Control System (ICS) in the absence of momentary glitches and outliers. In general, when a dataset is created for a study, the plant is run continuously under normal operating

conditions. The same has been done in this study for obtaining the data to create the models. However, when these models were tested on the plant when it was not running, unexpected outcomes were observed.

4. *Attack Detection Speed*: The speed with which a process anomaly is detected is of prime concern for the safety of the plant, but it is often ignored as a performance attribute [7]. Rapid detection allows for appropriate actions to be taken earlier, thereby mitigating the impact. Therefore, Time Taken for Detection (TTD) has been used as an important performance metric in this study, while highlighting its significance.

Organization: The remainder of this paper is organized as follows. The mathematical modelling of the two testbeds as systems is explained in Sect. 2. The attack detection framework in Sect. 3 briefly explains the working of the three detection techniques that form the focus of this paper. Following this, Sect. 4 defines the attacker profile while detailing the potential attack scenarios and their execution. The performance of the detection mechanisms is evaluated in Sect. 5, whereby the techniques are tested under normal and attack conditions. Based on the analysis of the results obtained, the conclusions that map to the contributions above, are presented in Sect. 6.

2 System Model

2.1 Two Testbeds: Our Playground

Research facilities with operational testbeds of prevalent cyber-physical systems have been utilised to implement the security strategies and test their capabilities. As mentioned earlier, these include a secure water treatment plant (SWaT) [8] and a water distribution plant (WADI) [9]. These are operational, scaled down plants that simulate the larger industrial infrastructure found in cities today. The physical process here is that of water flow, wherein it undergoes specific processes, for e.g., ultra-filtration, reverse osmosis, etc. The plants are divided into different stages, each carrying out a specific sub-process. The detailed workings of the testbeds are explained in papers [8,9].

2.2 System Models

Each of the two testbeds is treated as a multi-input, multi-output system, following the model-based approach. A system model represents the dynamics of a physical process using a mathematical formulation. Sub-space system identification techniques are used to obtain models of the following form, for a system with p control inputs (actuators) and m outputs (sensors):

$$\begin{cases} x_{k+1} = Ax_k + Bu_k + v_k, \\ y_k = Cx_k + \eta_k. \end{cases} \tag{1}$$

where k represents the time instance, $x \in \mathbb{R}^n$ is system state vector of n states, $A \in \mathbb{R}^{n \times n}$ is state-space matrix, $B \in \mathbb{R}^{n \times p}$ is the control matrix, $y \in \mathbb{R}^m$ is the vector of the measured outputs, $C \in \mathbb{R}^{m \times n}$ is measurement matrix, and $u \in \mathbb{R}^p$ denotes the system control input.

The state-space matrices A, B and C capture the system dynamics and can be used to find a specific system state given an initial state. The sensor and process noise vectors are represented by η_k and v_k, respectively.

2.3 Validation of the System Models

It is necessary to validate the models created for each of the systems. For this, the state-space matrices from the system identification process are applied and the estimates for the output of the system are obtained. These modelled values and real-time sensor measurements are then compared. The difference between the measured sensor values and estimates is considered using the root mean square error (RMSE). The RMSE value for N readings is given as follows:

$$RMSE = \sqrt{\frac{\sum_{i=1}^{N} (y_i - \hat{y}_i)^2}{N}}.$$

where y_i is the actual i-th sensor reading, and $\hat{y}_i$ is the i-th model estimate.

The accuracy of the system identification-based model for 6 sensors in the SWaT testbed is shown in Table 1 as an example, and it can be seen this model has high accuracy. In control theory literature, models with accuracy as high as 70% are considered a sufficiently precise approximation of real system dynamics [10, 11].

Table 1. Validating SWAT model obtained from sub-space system identification.

Sensor	FIT101	LIT101	LIT301	FIT301	LIT401	FIT401
RMSE	0.0363	0.2867	0.2561	0.0200	0.2267	0.0014
(1-RMSE) * 100%	96.3670	71.3273	74.3869	98.0032	77.3296	99.8593

3 Attack Detection Framework

This work focuses on detecting attacks on sensors, primarily by validating the incoming readings. This is done by (1) estimating the sensor output using the system model, and (2) examining the residual between the actual and estimated values and verifying the source of the sensor readings. The second step is in turn done using the three different detectors (CUSUM, Bad-Data and *NoisePrint*) for comparison.

System Model and Estimation: The concept of creating system models is explained in the previous section. These can be obtained either using data-based techniques or from first principles [12–14]. Using the system model, it is possible to estimate the states of the system and ultimately predict the output from a sensor applying Eq. 1. At a time instance k, a residual vector (r_k) is calculated by taking the difference between the sensor measurements (y_k) and estimated sensor output $(\hat{y}_k)$, which is given as:

$$r_k = y_k - \hat{y}_k. \tag{2}$$

For the residual, the hypothesis testing is for $\mathcal{H}_0$, the *normal mode* (no attacks), and $\mathcal{H}_1$, the *faulty mode* (with attacks). The residuals are obtained using this data and the state estimates. The two hypotheses are stated as follows:

$$\mathcal{H}_0 : \begin{cases} E[r_k] = 0, \\ E[r_k r_k^T] = \Sigma, \end{cases} \text{ or } \mathcal{H}_1 : \begin{cases} E[r_k] \neq 0, \\ E[r_k r_k^T] \neq \Sigma. \end{cases}$$

Threshold-Based Detection: To detect the presence of an attack, the residual vector is tested against a predefined threshold designed for a particular false alarm rate. A threshold is created for the residual distribution, and while testing the model against the actual data from the plant, an attack is declared if the residual values exceed that threshold:

$$|r_k| > \tau, \, Alarm = \text{TRUE} \tag{3}$$

where τ is the threshold and $|r_k|$ is the absolute value of the residual. There have been studies on optimizing the parameters of different stateful and stateless detectors [13, 14]. Next, the three attack detection techniques deployed in this study are outlined.

3.1 Cumulative Sum (CUSUM) Detector

The standard CUSUM [15] procedure is explained using the following equations.

CUSUM: $S_{0,i}^- = 0, \; S_{0,i}^+ = 0, \; \tilde{k}_i^+ = 0, \; \tilde{k}_i^- = 0,$

$$\begin{cases} S_{k,i}^+ = \max(0, S_{k-1,i}^+ + r_{k,i} - \bar{T}_i - \kappa_i), & \text{if } S_{k-1,i}^+ \leq \tau_i^+, \\ S_{k,i}^+ = 0 \text{ and } \tilde{k}_i^+ = \tilde{k}_i^+ + 1, & \text{if } S_{k-1,i}^+ > \tau_i^+. \end{cases} \tag{4}$$

$$\begin{cases} S_{k,i}^- = \min(0, S_{k-1,i}^- + r_{k,i} - \bar{T}_i + \kappa_i), & \text{if } S_{k-1,i}^- \geq \tau_i^-, \\ S_{k,i}^- = 0 \text{ and } \tilde{k}_i^- = \tilde{k}_i^- + 1, & \text{if } S_{k-1,i}^- < \tau_i^-. \end{cases} \tag{5}$$

Design parameters: bias $\kappa_i > 0$ and threshold $\tau_i > 0$.
Output: $alarm(s) = \tilde{k}_i^+ + \tilde{k}_i^-$.

From Eqs. 4–5, it can be observed that the CUSUM values $S_{k,i}^+$ and $S_{k,i}^-$ accumulate the distance measured $r_{k,i}$ over time to measure how far the values of the residual are from the target mean ($\bar{T}_i$). The slack variable κ can be adjusted to tune this window for error. The parameters are chosen suitably to achieve a required false alarm rate $\mathcal{A}_i^*$.

3.2 Bad-Data Detector

The Bad-Data detector is widely used in the CPS security literature [16].

Bad-Data Procedure:

$$\text{If } |r_{k,i}| > \alpha_i, \; \tilde{k}_i = k, \; i \in \mathcal{I}. \tag{6}$$

Design parameter: threshold $\alpha_i > 0$.
Output: alarm time(s) $\tilde{k}_i$.

Using the Bad-Data detector, an alarm is triggered if distance measure, taken as $|r_{k,i}|$, exceeds the threshold α_i. Analogous to the CUSUM procedure, the parameter α_i is selected to satisfy a required false alarm rate $\mathcal{A}_i^*$.

3.3 *NoisePrint* (Machine Learning-based Device Fingerprinting)

NoisePrint is a sensor fingerprinting technique that makes use of a Support Vector Machine (SVM) [3]. It is based on the principle that when the system is in steady state [17], the residual vector of its model is a function of sensor and process noise. Therefore, it is possible to extract these sensor and process noise characteristics of the given ICS from the residual vectors. Following this, pattern recognition techniques such as machine learning are applied on the residual vectors to fingerprint the given sensor and process.

The proposed scheme begins with data collection which is then divided into smaller chunks to extract a set of time domain and frequency domain features. Features are combined and labeled with a sensor ID. A machine learning algorithm is used for classifying sensors based on their noise profiles. For more details, an interested reader is referred to [3, 18].

4 Threat Model

Since the attacks taken into consideration for this work are on sensors, a few assumptions have been made about the attacker. These are given as follows:

1. The attacker has access to $y_{k,i} = C_i x_k + \eta_{k,i}$ (i.e., the i-th sensor measurements at the kth time instance).
2. The attacker has the knowledge about the system dynamics, the state-space matrices, the control inputs and outputs, and the implemented detection measure.

Tables 2 and 3 show the attacks carried out on SWaT and WADI. Based on their execution, these can be classified as follows:

– *Single-point Attack*—these types of attacks target a single point in the system, manipulating its value and/or disrupting its communication link.
– *Multi-point Attack*—in these types of attacks, multiple points are targeted simultaneously.
– *Stealthy Attack*—these are the attacks wherein the data value of a sensor is altered very slightly, which makes it difficult to detect the abnormality.

The single- and multi-point attacks, in turn, can be single-stage or multi-stage. In single-stage attacks, the attack points are limited to one particular stage of the plant, whereas in multi-point attacks, the target points can be spread across several stages. In real scenarios, these are dependent on the attacker's competence, extent of access and intentions.

The attacks mentioned in Tables 2 and 3 simulate data injection attacks of two kinds:

– *Bias Injection Attack*: The attacker's goal in this type of attack is to deceive the control system by sending incorrect sensor readings. The attack vector in such a scenario can be defined as:

$$\bar{y}_k = y_k + \delta_k, \tag{7}$$

where $\bar{y}_k$ is the general sensor measurement at a time instance k, y_k is the actual sensor reading and δ_k is the biased value injected by the attacker.

For e.g., Atk-2-s in Table 2 is a simple attack wherein a bias is added to the LIT-101 reading such that the value read by the PLC is changed from the original, which is 659 mm, to a spoofed value of 850 mm. Similarly, in Atk-2-w in Table 3, the 2-FIT-001 value is changed from its original 0 m³/h to a 1.5 m³/h, and the control actions taken by the PLC are based on this fake value.

- *Stealthy Attack:* In this case, the attack vector δ_k for Eq. (7) is chosen in a way that it stays inconspicuous while using statistical detectors. This happens because in these types of attacks, the residual vector may not noticeably change or exceed the thresholds, which is necessary for statistical detectors to confirm an attack.

A example of a stealthy attack is Atk-1-s from Table 2. In this attack, the reading of LIT-101 is originally 659 mm, and during the course of the attack, a small bias is repeatedly injected such that this value gradually increases by 1 mm every second.

Such attacks are operational technology (OT) attacks that aim to compromise the normal performance of the plant by manipulating sensor and/or actuator states. The SCADA system coupled with the SWaT and WADI testbeds provides an option of manually altering the sensor/actuator values that are being sent to the PLCs, and this func-

Table 2. List of attacks (SWaT): column 1 states the attack ID, and column 2 provides the details, wherein the '/' separates the system state before and during the attack.

Attack ID	Description (Initial state/Attack state)
Stage 1	
Atk-1-s	LIT101 = 659 mm/change level +1 mm/s
Atk-2-s	LIT101 = 659 mm/LIT101 = 850 mm
Atk-3-s	LIT101 = 659 mm/LIT101 = 210 mm
Atk-4-s	LIT101 = 679 mm/LIT101 = 700 mm
Atk-5-s	LIT101 = 1029 mm/LIT101 = 700 mm
Atk-6-s	LIT101 = 789 mm/LIT101 = 789 mm
Atk-7-s	LIT101 = 784 mm/LIT101 = 600 mm
Stage 3	
Atk-8-s	L < LIT301 < H/LIT301 = HH+
Atk-9-s	L < LIT301 < H/change level −1 mm/s
Atk-10-s	L < LIT301 < H/change level −0.5 mm/s
Atk-11-s	FIT301 = 0 m³/h/FIT301 = 2 m³/h
Atk-12-s	L < LIT301 < H/water leakage attack
Stage 4	
Atk-13-s	FIT401 = 0.48 m³/h/FIT401 = 0 m³/h
Atk-14-s	LIT401 < 1000 mm, P401 = ON/LIT401 = 1000 mm and P401 = ON
Atk-15-s	L < LIT401 < H, P301 = ON/LIT401 = 600 mm and P301 = ON
Atk-16-s	L < LIT401 < H/LIT401 < L
Atk-17-s	LIT401 = 1005 mm/LIT401 = 1005 mm

Table 3. List of attacks (WADI): column 1 states the attack ID, and column 2 provides the details, wherein the '/' separates the system state before and during the attack.

Attack ID	Description (Initial state/Attack state)
Atk-1-w	1-FIT-001 = 1.71 m^3/h/1-FIT-001 = 1.5 m^3/h
Atk-2-w	2-FIT-001 = 0 m^3/h/2-FIT-001 = 1.5 m^3/h
Atk-3-w	2-FIT-003 = 0 m^3/h/2-FIT-003 = 1 m^3/h
Atk-4-w	1-LT-001 = 55%/1-LT-001 = 80%
Atk-5-w	1-LT-001 = 40.21%/1-LT-001 = 40.21%
Atk-6-w	2-LT-002 = 46%/2-LT-002 = 65%
Atk-7-w	2-LT-002 = 71.2%/2-LT-002 = 71.2%

tion has been used to simulate some of the simple bias injection attacks. For the more complicated attacks, customised Python programs have been developed that gradually change the attack vector to simulate a stealthy attack. Custom-coded modules developed at iTrust Labs [19] have been used that are able to communicate with the LabVIEW-based[1] SCADA interface in order to launch the stealthy attacks.

5   Performance Evaluation

5.1   Performance Metrics

The precision and sensitivity of the attack detection method are part of the criteria to analyse its effectiveness. The following metrics have been used to assess the three procedures:

– True Positive Rate (TPR) and False Negative Rate (FNR)—The TPR refers to the number of times the method correctly raises alarms (predicts an attack) over the duration of the attack. The FNR is an alternate way of expressing the same metric:

$$FNR = 100\,\% - TPR$$

– False Positive Rate (FPR) or False Alarm Rate (FAR)—this refers to the number of times the method incorrectly raises alarms in the absence of any attack.
– Time Taken for Detection (TTD)—this refers to the time taken by the procedure to raise an alarm in the event of an attack.

The TPR of the technique is a direct indication of its attack detection accuracy and must be as high as possible. The FPR represents the tendency of the procedure to raise false alarms, which is extremely inconvenient in practical scenarios, and should be satisfactorily small. A high TPR is not very beneficial if the mechanism takes too long to detect the attack. This is because in a realistic sense, the CPS performs critical, large-scale

---

[1] Laboratory Virtual Instrument Engineering Workbench (LabVIEW) is a system-design software developed by National Instruments. For attack tool see: https://gitlab.com/gyani/NiSploit.

processes that influence the surrounding economy in multiple ways. A significant delay in the detection of an attack can be detrimental not only to the system itself, but also to its end-users. Therefore, the detection mechanism must have reasonable TTD.

In practical applications, there often exists a trade-off between a high TPR and a low FPR. A detection method may have a high FPR while managing to achieve a good TPR. Likewise, it is also possible to design for a low FPR but at the cost of missing some attacks, resulting in a low TPR. Hence, the two rates must always be balanced such that a satisfactory TPR is attained while having a feasible FPR.

5.2 Normal Operation

As emphasized earlier, attack detection mechanisms must be designed in a way such that they do not raise too many false alarms. Hence, the detection techniques were implemented on both the plants, and their performances were observed when the plants were under normal operation.

For both the plants, the thresholds for the CUSUM and Bad-Data detectors have been designed to allow an FPR of 5% (or less). This is done to account for the temporary aberrations caused by technical glitches or external disturbances, which often occur in practical industrial plants. Each detector has thresholds and design parameters dedicated to each sensor, which are presented in Tables 4 and 5. It can be seen in these tables that, for both plants, these two attack detection methods generate false alarms within a reasonable window around the designed limit.

Figure 1 shows the residual from the system identification-based model for the level sensor (2-LT-002) in WADI. It can be seen that it mostly remains below its Bad-Data threshold during normal operation, shown in Fig. 1a. Likewise, the CUSUM values also stay within the thresholds for 2-LT-002 under normal operation, as seen in Fig. 1b. This implies that the design of the Bad-Data and CUSUM thresholds is in accordance with the requirement and it is feasible to implement these detectors on the plants under normal operating conditions.

When tested on SWaT, *NoisePrint* performed very well, with low or zero FPRs for almost all of the sensors. However, in the case of WADI, the FPRs for most of the sensors were above the desired 5%. The sensors in WADI are known to be sensitive to disturbances from the environment, thus resulting in some faults in their measurements, and this could be the reason *NoisePrint* fails to perform well.

From these figures and tables, it can be concluded that the detection methods perform satisfactorily well on both the testbeds under normal operating conditions. The x-axis for all the figures is the time in seconds for which sensor data is plotted. However, it is to be noted that these figures are for demonstration purposes only and do not show the complete dataset. For the normal operation of the water plants, the dataset is collected for more than a week and the attack data ranges from 5–30 min for each attack [20]. The FPR is only shown for the normal data evaluations. As for the case of the attack evaluation table in the following section, the data used was recorded only when the sensors were under attack, and hence shows FNR only. The rate (TPR) is calculated using the number of alarms raised for the whole duration of the attack.

Table 4. False positives under normal operation in SWaT.

Sensor	FIT101	LIT101	FIT301	LIT301	FIT401	LIT401
CUSUM detector						
Threshold	0.0149	3.1168	0.2209	0.5529	0.0156	0.5674
κ	0.0074	0.3117	0.0276	0.1382	0.0028	0.1135
FAR	5.54%	5.19%	5.34%	4.65%	4.02%	4.03%
Bad Data detector						
Threshold	0.0205	1.4100	0.1184	0.4887	0.0108	0.4178
FAR	4.29%	5.32%	4.84%	4.56%	5.41%	5.42%
NoisePrint						
FAR	0%	1.29%	8.3%	2.44%	0%	0%

Table 5. False positives under normal operation in WADI.

Sensor	1-LT-001	2-LT-002	2-PIT-001	2-PIT-002	1-FIT-001	2-FIT-001	2-FIT-002	2-FIT-003
CUSUM detector								
Threshold	1.109	0.6534	8.6809	0.2107	0.2964	0.0995	0.311	1.2972
κ	0.3466	0.2042	0.8681	0.3511	0.0823	0.0829	0.0389	0.1081
FAR	4.61%	3.76%	5.01%	3.47%	4.29%	4.13%	4.93%	5.01%
Bad Data detector								
Threshold	1.122	0.7674	3.5104	0.7239	0.2063	0.3018	0.1548	0.487
FAR	4.40%	4.19%	4.08%	3.89%	4.64%	3.49%	4.56%	4.80%
NoisePrint								
FAR	13.04%	6.95%	21.74%	6.95%	6.08%	11.30%	4.34%	11.30%

5.3 Attack Detection

The three detection techniques were tested under different attack scenarios on both the plants. Tables 2 and 3 show the attacks carried out on SWaT and WADI, respectively. The residuals for the sensors from the system identification-based models were obtained and the detection techniques were applied while the plants were under attack. The performance metrics were computed for the different attacks on each of the testbeds and can be seen in Tables 6 and 7.

In the case of SWaT, it can be seen in Table 6 that the CUSUM and Bad-Data detectors perform well under a variety of bias injection attacks, like Atk-11-s, Atk-4-s and Atk-5-s. However, they fail to detect the stealthy attacks Atk-17-s and Atk-6-s. Whereas, *NoisePrint* is able to successfully detect the presence of all attacks, including the stealthy attacks, and demonstrates a comparable TPR for other cases. The attacks that report poor TPR while using CUSUM and Bad-Data thresholds can be detected better using *NoisePrint*. However, the superior performance of *NoisePrint* comes at the cost of speed of detection. The time taken by the CUSUM and Bad-Data detectors to confirm the occurrence of the attack is considerably less than that of *NoisePrint*, implying that they have a better TTD compared to *NoisePrint*.

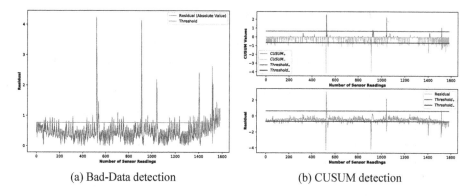

(a) Bad-Data detection   (b) CUSUM detection

Fig. 1. Statistical attack detection methods applied on the residual for level sensor (2-LT-002) estimates from WADI under normal operation. X-axis shows number of sensor reading sampled at 1 s intervals.

Figure 2 shows the residual when the level sensor (LIT-101) in SWaT is under a stealthy attack. In this attack, an attacker chooses to spoof the sensor measurement at the same value as the last known normal reading, thus deceiving the controller, while the real process state continues to progress differently. As seen in Figure 2a, the residual stays below the threshold during the stealthy attack. Similarly, in Figure 2b, it can be seen that the CUSUM values also always stay below the CUSUM thresholds. This shows that the stealthy attack could not be detected by either of the two detectors. However, as mentioned in Table 6 *NoisePrint* is able to detect this attack.

In the case of WADI, when the CUSUM detector is implemented on the residuals obtained from the system models, unsatisfactory TPRs are reported for all the attacks, as shown in Table 7. The Bad-Data detector performs reasonably well for attacks Atk-2-w and Atk-7-w, while *NoisePrint* shows a 100% TPR for attacks Atk-2-w, Atk-3-w and Atk-7-w. Both methods report poor TPRs for the other attacks. Similar to the case of SWaT, the TTD of *NoisePrint* is much higher than that of the Bad-Data detector.

These results show that while the statistical detectors, Bad-Data and CUSUM, are successfully able to confirm basic attacks such as bias injections, they fail to detect the more complicated stealthy attacks. This is expected because stealthy attacks are devised such that they do not tend to cause substantial changes to the residuals obtained from models, thereby ensuring the thresholds that determine the presence of an attack are not crossed. On the other hand, *NoisePrint* is able to identify such attacks, since the attacker may not be able to replicate the process and sensor noise, which form the basis of detection in *NoisePrint*. However, despite achieving better accuracy, *NoisePrint* falls behind in terms of detection speed.

Given the nature and performance of the detection mechanisms, the practical applicability of the methods can be challenged. The testbeds used in this work are small-scale and hence, obtaining complete system models for them was a feasible task. This might not be the case for actual industrial CPSs. A possible solution to this would be dividing the larger plants into several sub-stages (based on the processes taking place) and having multiple models corresponding for each sub-system.

Table 6. Attack detection performance on SWaT testbed.

Attack	NoisePrint			CUSUM			Bad Data		
	TPR	FNR	TTD (s)	TPR	FNR	TTD (s)	TPR	FNR	TTD (s)
Single point attacks									
Atk-8-s	85.72%	14.28%	121.22	17.46%	82.54%	2	16.75%	83.25%	2
Atk-9-s	14.50%	85.50%	179	88.15%	11.85%	2	93.18%	6.82%	2
Atk-10-s	80.64%	19.35%	130.09	56.30%	43.70%	5	58.48%	41.52%	3
Atk-11-s	87.50%	12.50%	89.59	100%	0%	1	100%	0%	1
Atk-12-s	63.63%	36.37%	117.83	95.42%	4.58%	6	96.64%	3.36%	6
Atk-1-s	88.88%	11.12%	32.48	91.16%	8.83%	2	91.34%	8.66%	1
Atk-2-s	67.56%	32.44%	46.90	85.08%	14.92%	1	78.02%	21.98%	1
Atk-3-s	90.91%	9.09%	35.25	98.92%	1.08%	1	99.08%	0.92%	1
Atk-7-s	88.24%	11.76%	57.35	77.58%	22.42%	1	60.62%	39.38%	1
Atk-13-s	55%	45%	44.43	32.82%	67.18%	2	13.94%	86.06%	2
Atk-16-s	86.21%	13.79%	56.26	6.21%	93.79%	1	6.32%	93.68%	1
Multi-point attacks									
Atk-14-s	81.82%	18.18%	125.59	16.32%	83.68%	1	6.76%	93.24%	1
Atk-15-s	77.78%	22.22%	105.3	54.68%	45.32%	2	99.64%	0.36%	2
Atk-4-s	94.73%	5.26%	35.59	99.66%	0.34%	1	100%	0%	1
Atk-5-s	90.47%	9.53%	44.50	99.68%	0.32%	1	100%	0%	1
Stealthy attacks									
Atk-17-s	80%	20%	67.03	0%	100%	**ND**	0%	100%	**ND**
Atk-6-s	75%	25%	174.84	0%	100%	**ND**	0%	100%	**ND**

Table 7. Attack detection performance on WADI (System identification model).

Attack	NoisePrint			CUSUM			Bad Data		
	TPR	FNR	TTD (s)	TPR	FNR	TTD (s)	TPR	FNR	TTD (s)
Single point attacks									
Atk-1-w	25%	75%	100	7.89%	92.11 %	1	21.74 %	78.26 %	1
Atk-2-w	100%	0%	50	51.28 %	48.72 %	2	91.11 %	8.89 %	2
Atk-3-w	100%	0%	50	22.22 %	77.78 %	1	13.16 %	86.84 %	1
Atk-4-w	20.51%	79.49%	150	1.81 %	98.19 %	1	3.59 %	96.41 %	1
Atk-6-w	56.25%	43.75%	100	17.67 %	82.33 %	1	32.49 %	67.51 %	1
Stealthy attacks									
Atk-5-w	19.44%	80.56%	200	1.40 %	98.60 %	2	2.51 %	97.49 %	1
Atk-7-w	100%	0%	50	45.79 %	54.21 %	3	94.02 %	5.98 %	1

In the case of *NoisePrint*, its longer detection time might render it less efficient when applied to some industrial CPSs, such as power grids, which require immediate response during attacks or anomalies. However, its accuracy is an important advantage when it comes to large systems with several sensors, and the method is still be applicable to CPSs wherein the attacks could take a longer time to cause any physical harm.

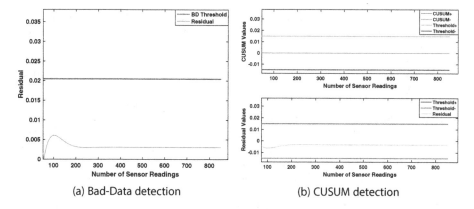

(a) Bad-Data detection   (b) CUSUM detection

Fig. 2. Statistical attack detection methods (Bad-Data and CUSUM) applied on the residual for level sensor (LIT-101) estimates from SWaT under stealthy attack

6   Conclusions

From the model validation results, it is understood that the models generated using well-established system identification algorithms perform reasonably well. An important insight is that obtaining a normal reference system model for the plants and sensors sensitive to environmental disturbances (e.g., for the WADI testbed in this study) is a non-trivial task. It is deduced that bias injection attacks on sensors that are quite similar to faults can be easily detected using statistical techniques like Bad-Data and CUSUM detectors. However, it is observed that advanced stealthy attacks require more sophisticated detection techniques, like *NoisePrint*. From the various tests carried out on the plants, it is concluded that while detection methods must be able to demonstrate accuracy, their attack detection speed is also a crucial metric for critical CPSs.

Acknowledgements. This work was supported by the SUTD start-up research grant SRG-ISTD-2017-124. The authors thank the reviewers for their comments. The authors express their gratitude to the iTrust research centre at Singapore University of Technology and Design for their research facilities, which have been extensively used in this work.

References

1. Cardenas, A., Amin, S., Lin, Z., Huang, Y., Huang, C., Sastry, S.: Attacks against process control systems: risk assessment, detection, and response. In: 6th ACM Symposium on Information. Computer and Communications Security, pp. 355–366 (2011)
2. Ahmed, C.M., Zhou, J.: Challenges and opportunities in CPS security: a physics-based perspective. IEEE Secur. Priv. (2020)
3. Ahmed, C.M., et al.: NoisePrint: attack detection using sensor and process noise fingerprint in cyber physical systems. In: AsiaCCS 18, pp. 483–497. ACM (2018)
4. Rocchetto, M., Tippenhauer, N.O.: On attacker models and profiles for cyber-physical systems. In: Askoxylakis, I., Ioannidis, S., Katsikas, S., Meadows, C. (eds.) ESORICS 2016. LNCS, vol. 9879, pp. 427–449. Springer, Cham (2016). https://doi.org/10.1007/978-3-319-45741-3_22

5. Krotofil, M., Gollmann, D.: Industrial control systems security: what is happening? In: 2013 11th IEEE International Conference on Industrial Informatics (INDIN), pp. 664–669, July 2013

6. Shoukry, Y., Martin, P., Yona, Y., Diggavi, S., Srivastava, M.: PyCRA: physical challenge-response authentication for active sensors under spoofing attacks. In: CCS 15, pp. 1004–1015. ACM (2015)

7. Mitchell, R., Chen, I.-R.: A survey of intrusion detection techniques for cyber-physical systems. ACM Comput. Surv. (CSUR) 46(4), 1–29 (2014)

8. SWaT: Secure Water Treatment Testbed (2015). https://itrust.sutd.edu.sg/wp-content/uploads/sites/3/2015/11/Brief-Introduction-to-SWaT_181115.pdf

9. Ahmed, C.M., Palleti, V.R., Mathur, A.P.: WADI: a water distribution testbed for research in the design of secure cyber physical systems. In: CPS Week. CySWATER 2017, pp. 25–28. ACM, 2017

10. Wei, X., Verhaegen, M., van Engelen, T.: Sensor fault detection and isolation for wind turbines based on subspace identification and Kalman filter techniques. Int. J. Adapt. Control Signal Process. 24(8), 687–707 (2010). https://doi.org/10.1002/acs.1162

11. Ahmed, C.M., Murguia, C., Ruths, J.: Model-based attack detection scheme for smart water distribution networks. In: Proceedings of the 2017 ACM on Asia Conference on Computer and Communications Security. ASIA CCS 2017, pp. 101–113. ACM, New York (2017). https://doi.org/10.1145/3052973.3053011

12. Qadeer, R., Murguia, C., Ahmed, C.M., Ruths, J.: Multistage downstream attack detection in a cyber physical system. In: Katsikas, S.K., et al. (eds.) CyberICPS/SECPRE -2017. LNCS, vol. 10683, pp. 177–185. Springer, Cham (2018). https://doi.org/10.1007/978-3-319-72817-9_12

13. Murguia, C., Ruths, J.: Characterization of a CUSUM model-based sensor attack detector. In: 2016 IEEE 55th Conference on Decision and Control (CDC), pp. 1303–1309, December 2016

14. Urbina, D.I., et al.: Limiting the impact of stealthy attacks on industrial control systems. In: Proceedings of the 2016 ACM SIGSAC Conference on Computer and Communications Security, pp. 1092–1105. ACM (2016)

15. Montgomery, D.: Introduction to Statistical Quality Control. Wiley, Hoboken (2009)

16. Liu, T., Gu, Y., Wang, D., Gui, Y., Guan, X.: A novel method to detect bad data injection attack in smart grid. In: 2013 IEEE Conference on Computer Communications Workshops (INFOCOM WKSHPS), pp. 49–54. IEEE (2013)

17. Aström, K.J., Wittenmark, B.: Computer-Controlled Systems, 3rd edn. Prentice-Hall Inc., Upper Saddle River (1997)

18. Ahmed, C.M., Zhou, J., Mathur, A.P.: Noise matters: using sensor and process noise fingerprint to detect stealthy cyber attacks and authenticate sensors in CPS. In: Proceedings of the 34th Annual Computer Security Applications Conference, pp. 566–581 (2018)

19. Adepu, S., Mishra, G., Mathur, A.: Access control in water distribution networks: a case study. In: 2017 IEEE International Conference on Software Quality, Reliability and Security (QRS), pp. 184–191, July 2017

20. Palleti, V.R., Mishra, V.K., Ahmed, C.M., Mathur, A.: Can replay attacks designed to steal water from water distribution systems remain undetected? ACM Trans. Cyber Phys. Syst. (2020)

Quantitative Information Security Vulnerability Assessment for Norwegian Critical Infrastructure

Yi-Ching Liao[✉]

Secure-NOK AS, Oslo, Norway
yi-ching.liao@securenok.com
https://www.securenok.com

Abstract. A single information security vulnerability exploitation within Norwegian critical infrastructure can have a significant impact on Norwegian society, even causing cascading effects on other countries. Therefore, it is essential to conduct a quantitative vulnerability assessment to secure the weakest link. However, quantifying vulnerabilities to the entire Norwegian critical infrastructure has not been properly conducted in the literature. Defining the sectors responsible for or involved in providing vital functions in Norwegian society as the scope, we propose a methodology of six processes to conduct a quantitative vulnerability assessment by integrating the information from three sources: (1) the regional Internet registry, (2) the banner crawlers, and (3) the vulnerability database. We present and visualize the results of the vulnerability assessment from four different aspects: (1) vulnerability, (2) window of exposure, (3) impact, and (4) exploitability. Based on the results, we can easily identify power supply and transport as the weakest link. Compared to the entire country, the vital societal functions are better secured. Such assessment should be conducted continuously and automatically by specified public authorities to identify, classify, quantify, and prioritize the time-varying vulnerabilities.

Keywords: Critical infrastructure · Quantitative information security vulnerability assessment · Norway

1 Introduction

Information security vulnerabilities are continuously growing, from 6,447 vulnerabilities in 2016 to 17,308 vulnerabilities in 2019, according to the statistics from the National Vulnerability Database (NVD) [11]. A single vulnerability exploitation within Norwegian critical infrastructure, which is essential for the maintenance of vital societal functions [1], can lead to cascading impacts across sectors in Norway or even across national borders [15]. However, the sectors responsible for or involved in providing vital functions (e.g., power supply, transport, etc.)

© Springer Nature Switzerland AG 2020
A. Rashid and P. Popov (Eds.): CRITIS 2020, LNCS 12332, pp. 31–43, 2020.
https://doi.org/10.1007/978-3-030-58295-1_3

in Norwegian society have different capacities for identifying time-varying vulnerabilities. To secure the weakest link, it is essential to conduct a quantitative vulnerability assessment for Norwegian critical infrastructure.

After identifying the research gap in Sect. 2, we demonstrate the different definitions of critical infrastructure and define the scope for quantitative vulnerability assessment in Sect. 3. Afterwards, we describe the methodology of six processes for conducting a quantitative vulnerability assessment in Sect. 4, and present and visualize the results from four different aspects in Sect. 5. Finally, we address the research limitations in Sect. 6, and conclude and identify the future work in Sect. 7.

2   Related Work

Quantifying vulnerabilities to the entire Norwegian critical infrastructure has not been properly conducted in the literature. Defining vulnerability as "a measure of system susceptibility to threat scenarios", Ezell [3] quantified vulnerability by measuring deterrence, detection, delay, and response. However, the proposed model was only applied to a medium-sized clean water system. Describing vulnerability as "a susceptibility to threats and hazards that substantially will reduce the ability of the system to maintain its intended function", Holmgren [5] proposed a framework for quantitative vulnerability assessment based on the studies from Swedish Defence Research Agency. Nevertheless, the suggested framework was only applied to electric power delivery.

Genge and Enăchescu [4] proposed a Shodan-based vulnerability assessment tool, which verifies the feasibility of integrating Shodan, Common Vulnerabilities and Exposures (CVE), and Common Vulnerability Scoring System (CVSS) for vulnerability assessment. However, the proposed tool was only applied to 12 Class C networks assigned to universities, telecommunications operators, railway systems, a bank, and a power company. To fill up the identified research gap, we follow the definition from National Institute of Standards and Technology (NIST), which specifies vulnerability as "weakness in an information system, system security procedures, internal controls, or implementation that could be exploited or triggered by a threat source" [10], and conduct a quantitative vulnerability assessment for Norwegian critical infrastructure.

3   Definitions and Sectors of Critical Infrastructure

The definition of critical infrastructure varies [15]. European Union defines critical infrastructure as "an asset, system or part thereof located in Member States which is essential for the maintenance of vital societal functions, health, safety, security, economic or social well-being of people, and the disruption or destruction of which would have a significant impact in a Member State as a result of the failure to maintain those functions" [1]. The selection of critical infrastructure sectors varies between countries as well. The most commonly selected critical infrastructure sectors include: energy, information and communications technology, transportation, health, water, finance and banking, government, food supply and distribution, chemical industry, public safety, law enforcement, nuclear sector, dams and flood defense, critical manufacturing, defense industry, and space sector [15].

Norway defines critical infrastructure as "the facilities and systems which are necessary to maintain or recover vital societal functions". Additionally, Norway describes vital societal functions as "the functions which are necessary to meet the societal basic needs and the population's sense of security" [2] or "the functions that society could not cope without for seven days or less without this threatening the safety and/or security of the population" [14]. Compared with other countries, Norway does not regard the space sector and the defense industry as critical infrastructure sectors [15]. Following these definitions, we determine these sectors as the scope to conduct a quantitative vulnerability assessment for Norwegian critical infrastructure.

4 Methodology

We follow six processes for conducting a quantitative vulnerability assessment for Norwegian critical infrastructure, which are explained as follows:

4.1 Summarize the Sectors Responsible for Vital Societal Functions

Norwegian Directorate for Civil Protection (DSB) has defined 14 vital societal functions and listed 126 sectors responsible for or involved in providing vital functions in Norwegian society [14]. We utilize these vital societal functions for further analysis and comparison in Subsect. 4.6 and employ the listed sectors as search keywords to retrieve sector-relevant IP addresses from the regional Internet registry in Subsect. 4.2.

4.2 Retrieve Sector-Relevant IP Addresses from Réseaux IP Européens (RIPE)

Réseaux IP Européens Network Coordination Centre (RIPE NCC) is the regional Internet registry which serves Europe, the Middle East, and parts of Central Asia. The RIPE NCC website [16] provides full-text search which enables us to use the sector names in Subsect. 4.1 as search terms to search over the RIPE database object data. For IP address retrieval, we search over only the full text of the "inetnum" database object, which specifies one or more IPv4 addresses.

Among the 126 sectors listed by DSB, there are 18 general terms, such as infrastructure owners, system owners, providers, and private businesses, which cannot be utilized as search terms. For sectors like regional health authorities, we extend the search terms to "Helse Sør-Øst RHF", "Helse Vest RHF", "Helse Midt-Norge RHF", and "Helse Nord RHF" based on publicly available information [8]. Another example is about the power and grid companies. We broaden the search scope with 143 search terms according to the lists of the largest Norwegian power and grid companies [12].

In case of no results found, we look up the domain name holder's information in the Norwegian domain registration directory service [13] and use the holder's information as the search term to search over the full text of the RIPE "inetnum" database object. If no results found again, we utilize the website's IP address if available. As a result, we retrieve 1,202,124 IP addresses from RIPE, which are utilized in Subsect. 4.4 for mapping with the vulnerable IP addresses.

For a comprehensive mapping, we generate tabular data with six fields: IP address, "netname", "descr", "org-name", sector name, and vital societal function. The "netname" attribute, which is the combination of letters, digits, and the underscore or hyphen character, represents the name of a range of IP addresses. The attribute "descr" and "org-name" specify the description and the name of the organization respectively. The name of the organization can be found in the "org-name" attribute if in American Standard Code for Information Interchange (ASCII) character encoding. If non-ASCII, the name of the organization can be stored in the "descr" attribute. Therefore, in addition to IP address, we can utilize the combination of "netname", "descr", and "org-name" attributes for extensive mapping with the vulnerable IP addresses in Subsect. 4.4.

4.3   Search Vulnerable IP Addresses Through Shodan

In this paper, we employ Shodan to search vulnerable IP addresses in Norway. Shodan, unlike the traditional web search engines, gathers the content of the banners instead of merely web pages. The banner, which describes the services on a device [6], can be utilized for vulnerability assessment. CVE Identifiers (CVE IDs) represent the publicly known vulnerabilities, and the Shodan crawlers store CVE IDs as property if the service is regarded as vulnerable. In addition to searching vulnerable IP addresses, we employ CVE IDs to correlate the severity of vulnerabilities in Subsect. 4.5.

For vulnerability assessment, we first downloaded all CVE IDs from the MITRE Corporation [9] on March 26th, 2020. We used these CVE IDs to get the total number of vulnerable IP addresses in Norway through Shodan from March 26th to 30th, 2020. The result shows Norwegian IP addresses are regarded as vulnerable to 1,598 CVE IDs. Knowing the publicly known vulnerabilities in Norway, we utilized these CVE IDs to download the results of vulnerable IP addresses into JavaScript Object Notation (JSON) files through Shodan from March 30th to April 2nd, 2020. Each JSON file contains the banners and other meta-data [6], from which we filtered out two fields: IP address and the organization which owns the IP address. As a result, we have 739,933 records with three fields: CVE ID, IP address, and organization, which show 431 organizations and 32,519 IP addresses in Norway are regarded as vulnerable by Shodan.

Even though Shodan provides the information about the organization which owns the IP address, we retrieve the "netname", "descr" and "org-name" attributes from RIPE for comprehensive mapping with the sector-relevant IP addresses in Subsect. 4.4. As a result, we generate tabular data with four fields:

vulnerable IP address, "netname", "descr", and "org-name". The combination of "netname", "descr", and "org-name" attributes enables us to retrieve the corresponding vital societal function.

4.4 Mapping the IP Addresses and the Attribute Combination Between RIPE and Shodan

To understand the scope of vulnerable IP addresses owned by the sectors responsible for vital societal functions in Norway, we map the 1,202,124 IP addresses retrieved from RIPE in Subsect. 4.2 with the 32,519 IP addresses regarded as vulnerable by Shodan in Subsect. 4.3. There are 496 IP addresses owned by the sectors responsible for or involved in providing vital functions in Norwegian society with 632 distinct CVE IDs.

For an extensive mapping, we utilize the combination of "netname", "descr", and "org-name" attributes to retrieve the vital societal functions from the tabular data in Subsect. 4.2 and the vulnerable IP addresses with corresponding CVE IDs from the tabular data in Subsect. 4.3. As a result, we generate tabular data with three fields: vulnerable IP address, vital societal function, and CVE ID. There are 540 vulnerable IP addresses with 12 different vital societal functions and 671 distinct CVE IDs.

4.5 Correlate the Vulnerability Published Dates and Scores from NVD

CVE ID, which represents each publicly known vulnerability, can be utilized to correlate information provided by NVD. For further analysis and comparison in Subsect. 4.6, we utilize the 1,598 CVE IDs in Subsect. 4.3 to retrieve the published date, the CVSS impact subscore, and exploitability subscore from NVD. Even though the current version of CVSS is 3.1, not all CVE IDs have CVSS version 3.1 scores. Therefore, for a comprehensive analysis, we correlate CVSS version 2 scores instead.

To illustrate the window of exposure, we calculate the number of years between the CVE published date and March 26th, 2020, when we started to search vulnerable IP addresses through Shodan. To facilitate quantitative vulnerability assessment, we utilize the CVSS scores to demonstrate the severity of vulnerabilities. The CVSS base metric group, which defines the fundamental characteristics of a vulnerability, contains three impact metrics on the CIA triad: confidentiality, integrity, and availability. The three impact metrics measure the degree of loss of confidentiality, integrity, and availability into three levels: none, partial, and complete, if a vulnerability is exploited successfully. The CVSS base metric group includes another three metrics about exploitability: access vector, access complexity, and authentication metrics [7]. For an in-depth analysis in Subsect. 4.6, we retrieve impact and exploitability subscores instead of the overall score.

4.6   Analyze and Compare Between the Vital Societal Functions and the Whole Country

No records of vulnerable IP address found with two vital societal functions: financial services and electronic communication networks and services. The infeasibility of utilizing the general terms among the sectors listed by DSB (e.g., infrastructure owners and providers) as search terms for RIPE can lead to no records of vulnerable IP address found with electronic communication networks and services. For comparing between 12 vital societal functions, we analyze from the following four aspects: vulnerability (the count of CVE IDs), window of exposure (the number of years since the vulnerability has been published), impact (the CVSS impact subscore), and exploitability (the CVSS exploitability subscore). Moreover, we calculate the average count, years, and scores per vulnerable IP address to compare between 12 vital societal functions and the whole country. The major reason we choose to sum the CVSS subscores for comparison lies in the CVSS base equation "BaseScore = round_to_1_decimal(((0.6 * Impact) + (0.4 * Exploitability) $-$ 1.5) * f(Impact)); f(impact) $= 0$ if Impact $= 0$, 1.176 otherwise", which is the foundation of CVSS scoring that calculates a base score ranging from 0 to 10 [7]. The analysis and comparison can be further enhanced if the asset criticality is available in the future.

5   Results

The results of the quantitative vulnerability assessment for Norwegian critical infrastructure are presented as follows:

5.1   Vulnerability

The tabular data in Subsect. 4.4 summarizes 671 distinct CVE IDs in connection with vital societal functions, 41.99% of distinct CVE IDs in Norway. Table 1 enumerates the distinct count of CVE IDs between the vital societal functions in descending order. As is presented, power supply, transport, and governance and crisis management hold higher distinct count of CVE IDs than other vital societal functions. Figure 1 illustrates the average count of CVE IDs per vulnerable IP address between the vital societal functions with the whole Norway's average count: 22.62 as the outermost line. Note that we sort the vital societal functions according to DSB's categorization: (1) governability and sovereignty: governance and crisis management, defense; (2) security of the population: law and order, health and care, emergency services, ICT security in the civil sector, nature and the environment, and (3) societal functionality: security of supply, water and sanitation, power supply, transport, satellite-based services.

5.2   Window of Exposure

Table 2 provides the total number of years since the vulnerability has been published between the vital societal functions in descending order, which implies

Table 1. The distinct count of CVE IDs between the vital societal functions

Vital societal function	Distinct count of CVE IDs
Power supply	587
Transport	454
Governance and crisis management	237
Emergency services	218
Nature and the environment	176
Health and care	156
Water and sanitation	154
Security of supply	134
ICT security in the civil sector	88
Satellite-based services	72
Defense	71
Law and order	53

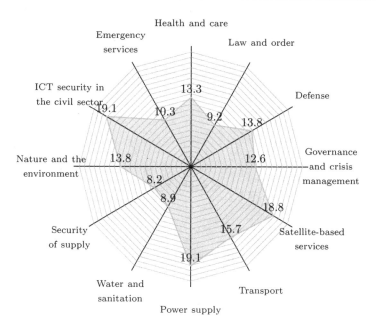

Fig. 1. The average count of CVE IDs per vulnerable IP address between the vital societal functions with the whole country's average count: 22.62 as the outermost line

the risk of vulnerabilities can be accepted or transferred among the vital societal functions. As the table suggests, power supply, transport, and nature and the environment have longer window of exposure than other vital societal functions. Figure 2 expresses the average number of years since the vulnerability has been published per vulnerable IP address between the vital societal functions with the whole Norway's average number of years: 246.33 as the outermost line, which suggests the publicly known vulnerabilities are mitigated quicker than general.

Note that in case of the system starting up after the vulnerability published date, the window of exposure will be overestimated.

Table 2. The total number of years since the vulnerability has been published between the vital societal functions

Vital societal function	Total number of years
Power supply	26124.8
Transport	16050.3
Nature and the environment	10605.9
Health and care	9795.3
Governance and crisis management	8338.8
Emergency services	7150.6
Water and sanitation	5458.5
Security of supply	4745.3
Satellite-based services	4020.6
ICT security in the civil sector	2254.4
Law and order	753.8
Defense	620.3

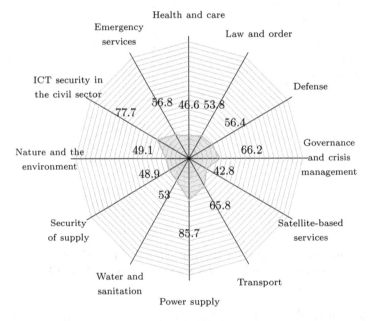

Fig. 2. The average number of years since the vulnerability has been published per vulnerable IP address between the vital societal functions with the whole country's average number of years: 246.33 as the outermost line

5.3   Impact

The total CVSS impact subscore of the vital societal functions is 102,769.6, 3.22% of the total CVSS impact subscore of vulnerable IP addresses in Norway, which is 3,193,033.8. Table 3 enumerates the sum of CVSS impact subscore between the vital societal functions in descending order, which indicates the degree of loss of confidentiality, integrity, and availability if a vulnerability is exploited successfully. As is observed, power supply, transport, and nature and the environment have higher impact caused by vulnerability exploitation than other vital societal functions. Figure 3 illustrates the average of CVSS impact subscore per vulnerable IP address between the vital societal functions with the whole Norway's average score: 196.37 as the outermost line. As the diagram suggests, the vital societal functions have less impact of vulnerability exploitation on the CIA triad than the entire country.

5.4   Exploitability

The total CVSS exploitability subscore of the vital societal functions is 198,373.2, 3.07% of the total CVSS exploitability subscore of vulnerable IP addresses in Norway, which is 6,464,958.2. Table 4 presents the sum of CVSS exploitability subscore between the vital societal functions in descending order. The CVSS exploitability subscore measures how the vulnerability is exploited, the complexity of the attack, and the number of times an attacker must authenticate for vulnerability exploitation [7]. Similar to the CVSS impact subscore, power supply, transport, and nature and the environment have higher exploitability than other vital societal functions. Figure 4 depicts the average of CVSS exploitability subscore per vulnerable IP address between the vital societal functions with the whole Norway's average score: 397.6 as the outermost line. As shown in the figure, the vital societal functions have less vulnerability exploitability than the entire country.

6   Discussions

We can easily identify power supply and transport as the weakest link of Norwegian critical infrastructure based on the results of the quantitative vulnerability assessment. Table 1 can also be utilized as a priority ranking of the vital societal functions for vulnerability remediation. Even though we cannot eliminate the possibility that broadening the search scope for the power and grid companies in Subsect. 4.2 may lead to more vulnerabilities found, the results demonstrate different capacities for vulnerability management between the vital societal functions. Therefore, it is essential to secure the weakest link by supporting critical infrastructure sectors to identify, classify, quantify, and prioritize the vulnerabilities.

We can simply understand the vulnerability level of critical infrastructure compared to the entire country through visualization. The results also imply

Table 3. The sum of CVSS impact subscore between the vital societal functions

Vital societal function	Sum of CVSS impact subscore
Power supply	25734.1
Transport	17537.3
Nature and the environment	13371.4
Health and care	12608.1
Satellite-based services	7396.0
Governance and crisis management	7378.0
Emergency services	6399.7
Water and sanitation	4700.2
Security of supply	4195.7
ICT security in the civil sector	2138.2
Defense	686.0
Law and order	624.9

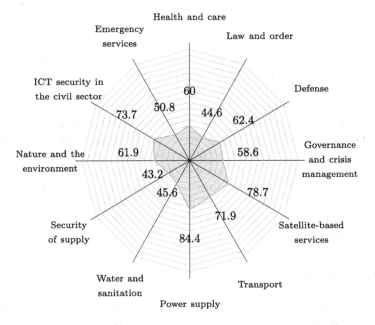

Fig. 3. The average of CVSS impact subscore per vulnerable IP address between the vital societal functions with the whole country's average score: 196.37 as the outermost line

the possibility of honeypot deployment within ICT security in the civil sector. Due to the time-varying vulnerabilities and the strong inter-dependencies between vital societal functions, it is important to conduct such quantitative vulnerability assessment continuously and automatically. Nevertheless, the process to retrieve sector-relevant IP addresses in Subsect. 4.2 can be one of the

Table 4. The sum of CVSS exploitability subscore between the vital societal functions

Vital societal function	Sum of CVSS exploitability subscore
Power supply	51612.5
Transport	33637.5
Nature and the environment	26111.7
Health and care	24495.6
Satellite-based services	15659.4
Governance and crisis management	13874.7
Emergency services	11110.6
Water and sanitation	7711.8
Security of supply	6729.2
ICT security in the civil sector	5009.3
Defense	1331.5
Law and order	1089.4

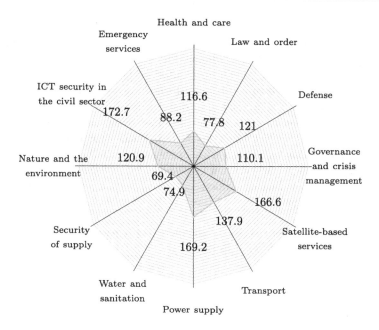

Fig. 4. The average of CVSS exploitability subscore per vulnerable IP address between the vital societal functions with the whole country's average score: 397.6 as the outermost line

automation challenges. Currently the full-text search is only provided through the RIPE NCC website [16], which hinders the process for automation.

As for the scope for quantitative vulnerability assessment, it is difficult to ensure the completeness and accuracy due to the general terms among the sectors listed by DSB. The infeasibility of utilizing these general terms as search terms for RIPE can lead to no records of vulnerable IP address found. Additionally, only Internet-facing devices registered in Norway are included for vulnerability assessment. Air-gapped devices or sector-relevant IP addresses registered outside of Norway are beyond the scope of this paper.

In addition to the scope for quantitative vulnerability assessment, it is also challenging to verify the completeness and accuracy of the vulnerable IP addresses found by Shodan. For instance, the deployment of honeypots can affect the accuracy of vulnerability assessment. Even though the processes for verifying the vulnerabilities [17] and identifying the honeypots [18] are still ongoing, it is better for specified public authorities to gather the content of the banners for vulnerability assessment to ensure the completeness and accuracy of assessment scope and results. Moreover, with the comprehensive list of assets and asset criticality, the analysis and comparison results based on the sum of CVSS subscores can be further enhanced.

7   Conclusions and Future Work

We propose a methodology of six processes for conducting a quantitative information security vulnerability assessment for Norwegian critical infrastructure, which denotes the potential for an automated system for quantitative vulnerability assessment. In the future, with the authorities' complete list of assets and asset criticality for Norwegian critical infrastructure, such automated system can facilitate the vulnerability management by identifying, classifying, quantifying, and prioritizing the vulnerabilities discovered. With visualized notification and remediation suggestion correlated with open-source intelligence to each sector, this automated system can continuously secure the weakest link of vital societal functions by providing dynamic security awareness for administrators and enabling proactive responses.

Acknowledgments. This research is conducted as a part of the CybWin project funded by the Research Council of Norway.

References

1. Council of the European Union: Council Directive 2008/114/EC, December 2008. http://data.europa.eu/eli/dir/2008/114/oj/eng
2. Departementenes Servicesenter, Informasjonsforvaltning: NOU 2006: 6, April 2006. https://www.regjeringen.no/no/dokumenter/nou-2006-6/id157408/
3. Ezell, B.C.: Infrastructure vulnerability assessment model (I-VAM). Risk Anal. Int. J. **27**(3), 571–583 (2007)
4. Genge, B., Enăchescu, C.: ShoVAT: Shodan-based vulnerability assessment tool for internet-facing services. Secur. Commun. Netw. **9**(15), 2696–2714 (2016). https://doi.org/10.1002/sec.1262
5. Holmgren, J.: A framework for vulnerability assessment of electric power systems. In: Murray, A.T., Grubesic, T.H. (eds.) Critical Infrastructure, pp. 31–55. Springer, Heidelberg (2007). https://doi.org/10.1007/978-3-540-68056-7_3
6. Matherly, J.: Complete guide to Shodan (2015)

7. Mell, P., Scarfone, K., Romanosky, S.: A Complete Guide to the Common Vulnerability Scoring System Version 2.0 (2007). https://www.first.org/cvss/v2/cvss-v2-guide.pdf
8. Ministry of Health and Care Services, Search Results: De regionale helseforetakene, November 2014. https://www.regjeringen.no/no/tema/helse-og-omsorg/sykehus/innsikt/nokkeltall-og-fakta---ny/de-regionale-helseforetakene/id528110/
9. MITRE Corporation: CVE List, March 2020. https://cve.mitre.org/data/downloads/index.html
10. National Institute of Standards and Technology (NIST): Glossary - vulnerability (2020). https://csrc.nist.gov/glossary/term/vulnerability
11. National Institute of Standards and Technology (NIST): National Vulnerability Database (NVD) - Statistics Results (2020). https://nvd.nist.gov/vuln/search/statistics?adv_search=false&form_type=basic&results_type=statistics&search_type=all
12. Nettbureau AS: Alle norske strømleverandører (2020). https://xn--strm-ira.no
13. Norid AS: The registry for Norwegian domain names (2020). https://www.norid.no/en/domeneoppslag/hvem-har-domenenavnet/
14. Norwegian directorate for civil protection (DSB): vital functions in society. Technical report (2017). https://www.dsb.no/globalassets/dokumenter/rapporter/kiks-2_januar.pdf
15. OECD: Good Governance for Critical Infrastructure Resilience (2019). https://doi.org/10.1787/02f0e5a0-en
16. RIPE NCC: RIPE Database Text Search (2020). https://apps.db.ripe.net/db-web-ui/fulltextsearch
17. Shodan: Facet Analysis (2020). https://beta.shodan.io/search/facet?query=net%3A0%2F0&facet=vuln.verified
18. Shodan: Honeypot Or Not? (2020). https://honeyscore.shodan.io/

Threat Modelling and Monitoring

A Systematic Literature Review of Information Sources for Threat Modeling in the Power Systems Domain

Engla Ling$^{(\boxtimes)}$ ⓘ, Robert Lagerström ⓘ, and Mathias Ekstedt ⓘ

Division of Network and Systems Engineering, KTH Royal Institute of Technology, Stockholm, Sweden
{englal,robertl,mekstedt}@kth.se

Abstract. Power systems are one of the critical infrastructures that has seen an increase in cyber security threats due to digitalization. The digitalization also affects the size and complexity of the infrastructure and therefore makes it more difficult to gain an overview in order to secure the entire power system from attackers. One method of how to gain an overview of possible vulnerabilities and security threats is to use threat modeling. In threat modeling, information regarding the vulnerabilities and possible attacks of power systems is required to create an accurate and useful model. There are several different sources for this information. In this paper we conduct a systematic literature review to find which information sources that have been used in power system threat modeling research. Six different information sources were found: expert knowledge, logs & alerts, previous research, system's state, vulnerability scoring & databases, and vulnerability scanners.

Keywords: Threat modeling · Power systems · Cyber security

1 Introduction

Power systems are a crucial part of any country's infrastructure. Without the access to electric power, the consequences can be severe, for example, hospitals being unable to operate. It is essential that the security of power systems is kept, especially when they are added to the communication infrastructure as part of digitalization. One method of ensuring the security of the power system is to gain an overview of its vulnerabilities by creating threat models. Threat modeling is a method of assessing security of systems and is further described in Sect. 3. Threat models are suitable for power systems because current security assessment techniques for enterprise IT environments might not be available for power systems. Power systems combine Information Technology (IT) with

Funded by Swedish Centre for Smart Grids and Energy Storage (SweGRIDS), the Swedish Civil Contingencies Agency's Resilient Information and Control Systems research centre as well as the European Union's H2020 research and innovation programme under the Grant Agreement No. 832907.

The original version of this chapter was revised: It has been changed to Open Access. The correction to this chapter is available at https://doi.org/10.1007/978-3-030-58295-1_8

A. Rashid and P. Popov (Eds.): CRITIS 2020, LNCS 12332, pp. 47–58, 2020.
https://doi.org/10.1007/978-3-030-58295-1_4

Operational Technology (OT) and there is often a combination of legacy and new techniques as well as equipment.

In this paper we find and discuss different information sources for vulnerability information when creating threat models for power systems. The aim is to contribute to the field of threat modeling in the power systems domain where finding reliable information to build a threat model is a crucial part of making sure that any conclusions drawn from the threat model is valid. It is not always clear how to find the information required to build a threat model and this article aims to aid in this process.

The research question is *What information sources have previously been used in research when generating threat models in the power systems domain?* The information sources have been found with a systematic literature review, i.e. a literature review where the process is carefully described so that the work can be repeated and avoid potential bias. This approach was chosen because there is a large amount of information in the research community, while in industry the created threat models are often not readily available being the potential security risk.

2   Related Work

The related work most closely related to this paper is "A review of cyber security risk assessment methods for SCADA systems" [8]. In that paper "SCADA" and "risk assessment" were used as keywords to find articles between 2004 and 2014. The authors found 24 articles according to these criteria. The difference between that study and this one is that they focused on all types of SCADA systems and on risk assessment. Cyber security risk assessment can be considered a broader term than threat modeling because the risk can be assessed by other means than with threat modeling. For example, it can be assessed by mathematical formulas. Another difference between cyber security risk assessment and threat modeling is that in risk assessment, the consequences of an attack are also taken into consideration. Even though the focus of that paper was not information sources, they presented it as part of their results. The authors found two different possible information sources, expert opinion and historical data. This is in contrast to this literature review paper where historical data was not mentioned in any of the articles and many more information sources were found. In addition, the different potential information sources were discussed in the article, indicating that the authors were aware that more than the two found by them exists.

Nazir et al. performed a survey for the techniques used to assess vulnerabilities of SCADA system [32]. Their survey was not a systematic literature review, but rather a collection of the most commonly used techniques including threat modeling. Some of the techniques that they discuss can be considered as information sources, for example using monitoring and test beds. They also discuss tools that can be used for gathering information. These tools are scanning tools, penetration testing, machine learning, Intrusion Detection System (IDS), Intrusion Prevention System (IPS), honey pots, Security information and event management (SIEM), ethical hacking and forensic science.

3   Threat Modeling

Threat modeling has many different definitions [45], but it is typically defined as a technique where the different security threats for a system are modelled. Often they are modelled in order to run simulations. This allows you to find potential future attacks. In this way one can make sure that the system is secure by using a model of the system instead of the actual system.

There are multiple ways of how to represent a threat model. For example, attack trees that were made popular by Schneier [37] shows a successful attack as the goal node of a tree with different attack steps leading up to that goal node. According to his paper, the attack goals, attacks against those goals and the values of the nodes, that is, the difficulty of the attacks, are required to build the attack tree. This type of information to build attack trees or any other type of threat model can be found by using several different information sources. For example, one can derive the information from vulnerability databases, industry experts or base it on previous attacks. It is important that this information source is reliable so that the resulting threat model can be trusted. The threat model may be used to make decisions of where to assign the most resources to protect the system depending on the result and any mistakes could be costly.

4   Method

The scope of this systematic literature review is defined by the search query that was used and the databases that were searched. The keywords were chosen based on the best of our knowledge on what would be the most inclusive but also include relevant articles. The following search query with keywords was used: (**"attack graph" OR "attack tree" OR "threat model*"**) **AND** (**"power system" OR "energy system" OR "power grid" OR "smart grid"**). The asterisk symbol means that the query will search for multiple variations of threat model, including "threat models" and "threat modeling".

The databases IEEE, Springer link, Web of Science, Science Direct and Scopus were used in this systematic literature review. In total 260 articles were found, and the specific search queries with results are shown below. The search was performed on the January 24th 2020.

IEEE 76 results after a search by Metadata. The metadata consists of abstract, title and indexing terms. Indexing terms are keywords that have been defined by the author.

Springer Link 415 results that were manually narrowed down to 17 results. This was because the title, abstract and keywords had to be filtered manually since Springer Link does not support that search request.

Web of Science 45 results after searching based on Topic, which includes title, abstract, author keywords, and Keywords Plus. Keywords plus are keywords generated automatically by an algorithm. The algorithm creates keywords based on the titles of the articles references.

Science Direct 9 results found based on Title, abstract or author-specified keywords.

Scopus 113 results based on their "TITLE-ABS-KEY" search.

After duplicates were removed from the final 260 articles, 146 of them remained. These articles were narrowed down to 44 articles according to the following inclusion criteria:

- The article must focus on cyber security.
- The article must include a threat model or the method of how one was constructed.
- The threat model must be in the power systems domain.
- The article must mention at least one information source that was used to create the threat model.
- The article must be written in English.

When the final 44 articles had been found, they were divided into categories of information source.

5   Information Sources

In Table 1 the information sources that were found in each article of the systematic literature review is summarized. This section describes and discusses the different information sources as found by this systematic literature review.

5.1   Expert Knowledge

From the results, 11 threat models were generated by using expert knowledge. Expert knowledge means that the developers have gained information from experts regarding, for example, what they believe to be the most likely attack scenarios. These experts are not necessarily experts in security but they are rather experts in the power systems domain. There is one exception and that is one article that used hacking knowledge [15]. The information was found by reading about attackers describing their goals.

Most often there is little information regarding the experts, how many they are and their credentials [25,36]. This makes it difficult to validate their results. Even if the experts are well known in terms of their credentials it can be difficult to know how much to stress each expert's opinion. In an article outside the scope of this review [22] the authors analyzed how to evaluate the correctness in expert knowledge judgement and how this could be used to weight in how much one considered a specific expert's opinion. This opens up the possibility of using expert knowledge, while prioritizing knowledge put forward by reliable experts.

There are some articles that discuss the method itself and these methods are the Delphi method [6,7], brainstorming [40] or allowing the experts to model themselves [18]. The Delphi method is a process of anonymous scoring followed by open discussions and results iteratively. The authors that used the brainstorming method saw a possible weak spot because of its dependency on who is participating from the stakeholders [40]. However, they claim that this was partly helped by the attending security experts. In the paper where the experts were allowed to model themselves they had some issues because the expert's modeling was not always in line with what could be translated easily to the threat modeling framework that they used [18].

One of the limitations of using industry experts is that they are often experts within one specific domain. This might make it difficult to model larger systems. This limitation was mentioned by [41]. In addition, they mentioned two other limitations. These are that the results are only valid during that instance and are constrained by the experts knowledge level. The authors expert knowledge reference group consisted of utility sector experts of Operational Technology (OT) systems. The experts were used to model the data flows. However, other information sources were used to create their attack graph because attack data was included in the framework that they used. In the threat modeling technique by Chen et al., a suggestion to this problem is presented where multiple smaller threat models are combined into one larger [5]. Each of the smaller threat models would be created by an industry expert in that domain.

Some articles use expert knowledge in combination with other information sources [15,17,41]. It can be easy to include expert knowledge because it may only be a question of asking an expert of their opinion. As seen in the articles of this systematic literature review, there are many different methods of how to include expert knowledge. This supports the fact that expert knowledge is easy to modify and adapt to your needs. However, one can question how to validate the results.

5.2 Logs and Alerts

A few articles use logged information as an information source. There are many different services that collect information about a system as logs and the resulting articles includes three of these different kinds of logs. One paper used information from archived IDS/IPS logs and alerts [15]. Another paper used event logs that they created themselves by running simulated attacks [14]. This might require a lot of time and skill to set up. An alternative could be to use historical data logs if that is available as Zhang et al. did [50]. Logs can be a very good source of information because there is often a very large amount of data that is collected. At the same time, it can be time consuming and require knowledge to go through all of the information.

5.3 Previous Research

The majority of articles found in this systematic literature review use previous research to find the different possible vulnerabilities or attacks on the systems that they model [4,13,16,19,23,26,28–30,34,46,52,53]. Previous research is also used in combination with other information sources [9–11,20,31,41]. This previous research can consist of research articles or published reports. In most cases it is not exactly specified where the authors have used previous research and where they have made assumptions. This makes it difficult to validate their results.

Table 1. Information sources for power system's threat models

Article	Expert Knowledge	Logs & Alerts	Previous Research	System's State	Vulnerability Scoring & Databases	Vulnerability Scanner
[6]	●					
[7]	●					
[40]	●					
[18]	●					
[41]	●		●		●	
[5]	●					
[25]	●					
[36]	●					
[15]	●	●		●		
[17]	●				●	●
[50]		●				
[14]		●				
[52]			●			
[46]			●			
[30]			●			
[26]			●			
[29]			●			
[23]			●			
[19]			●			
[16]			●			
[53]			●			
[4]			●			
[28]			●			
[13]			●			
[34]			●			
[20]			●	●		
[31]			●		●	
[10]			●		●	
[9]			●		●	
[11]			●		●	
[39]				●		
[38]				●		
[27]				●		
[51]					●	
[47]					●	
[43]					●	
[42]					●	
[48]					●	
[35]					●	●
[49]					●	
[2]					●	●
[1]					●	
[44]					●	
[12]					●	

Previous research is however a valid information source where it is referenced properly because the source has often been peer-reviewed before publication.

5.4   System's State

Five of the articles used the state of the system that they want to model to evaluate the vulnerabilities or potential attacks. The state of the system can be to for example analyze the security implementations [15,27,38,39], make a forensics analysis [38,39] or look at configuration files [20].

There was a large variation of the type of information used from the system and how they used it found in this review. When using a system's state as an information source, no other resource or information is required except the system itself. This makes the information source easy to use. However, it might take time to collect the appropriate information and experts to be able to analyze the results accurately.

5.5   Vulnerability Scoring and Databases

17 articles of this systematic literature review was found to use vulnerability scoring or databases as an information source. Some of the articles use a combination of the scoring systems with the databases and some only use one of them. The most common scoring system as found in this review is the Common Vulnerability Scoring System (CVSS)[1] [42,43,47,48,51]. The CVSS is a scoring system that was developed by and maintained by Forum of Incident Response and Security Teams (FIRST). The authors in [21], outside the scope of this review, found that using CVSS alone does not perform well as an information source for threat modeling. While the authors in [24] found that in general CVSS can be trusted. In addition, their results also showed that if one considers all of the systems vulnerabilities and not only those with the highest CVSS score, the results were much more reliable. Some papers found in this review use a combination of calculating their own CVSS scores with vulnerability databases or other information sources [9–11]. Another example of a scoring system is the Common Weakness Enumeration (CWE) is a category system that also calculates a score for the weaknesses or vulnerabilities[2] [35]. The CWE includes all software weaknesses and not only vulnerabilities.

There are multiple different vulnerabilities databases that aim to categorize and explain vulnerabilities for different systems and these can be used as information sources when modeling. The ones found in this review are the U.S. National Vulnerability Database (NVD)[3] [2,12,17,41,49], MITRE[4] [31,44], several CERTs databases[5,6,7] [1,12,44] as well as the Chinese databases Chinese National Vulnerability Database (CNNVD)[8] [41].

---

[1] https://www.first.org/cvss/ [accessed 28 April 2020].
[2] https://cwe.mitre.org/ [accessed 28 April 2020].
[3] https://nvd.nist.gov/ [accessed 28 April 2020].
[4] https://cve.mitre.org/cve/search_cve_list.html [accessed 28 April 2020].
[5] https://www.kb.cert.org/vuls/search/ [accessed 28 April 2020].
[6] https://www.cert.org.cn/ [accessed 28 April 2020].
[7] https://www.us-cert.gov/ics/monitors [accessed 28 April 2020].
[8] http://www.cnnvd.org.cn/ [accessed 28 April 2020].

The positive aspect of using this information as a source is that a lot of information is readily available. This information source can also adapt easily to changes. If one is constructing a threat model with this source, it is possible to quickly update the vulnerability information if the scoring or database change. One downside of using the vulnerability scoring and databases is that this information has the possibility of bias. This is because there are experts who use their experience and knowledge to estimate properties that give vulnerabilities a specific score. It is difficult to know exactly where the articles gain the information, they might phrase it as "vulnerabilities can be found in vulnerability databases, for example X,Y,Z". In these cases we assume that those are the databases used.

5.6   Vulnerability Scanner

A vulnerability scanner can automatically detect vulnerabilities within a system and three articles in this literature review used them as an information source [2, 17,35]. In all of these papers, the vulnerability scanner was used in combination with another information source. A scanner may require time to set up, but it provides a lot of information that can often already be analyzed by the tool itself. Similar to the information source of previous research, it is not always clear to what extent the vulnerability scanning has been used. Sometimes the articles will give examples of vulnerability scanning tools that may be used, and in this can the assumption is that those tools have actually been used.

6   Discussion

Similar to any systematic literature review work, there is the possibility of changing the database, keywords and inclusion criteria that is used. For example, Google Scholar and arXiv could have been searched as well. The downside of using a database, such as Google Scholar, is that it includes other work such as e.g. student thesis reports in addition to peer-reviewed research papers. If we would search the full text of articles and not only the title, abstract and keywords then the result does not only show many more articles, but these articles may not be relevant for the research question.

Another limitation of this work that exists because of the nature of a systematic literature review is that some articles will not be included in the results. For instance, the terms "risk assessment" [33], "SCADA" [3] may be used instead of the search terms in this systematic literature review. However, if those search terms were included the review would result in many irrelevant articles. There may also be other information sources being used other than those included in published research. These might be information sources used by threat models created in the industry.

Possible future work includes looking into the relations between the different information sources and how some of them may overlap or complement each other. It could also be to look into information sources that exist in other domains and use these in the power systems domain. Future work could also be to automatically keep this list of information sources up to date by utilizing the databases' API and some form of natural language processing solution. Planned future work is to use some of the found information sources to develop threat models for power systems.

7 Conclusion

In this article a systematic literature review was used as a method to find the different information sources that have previously been used in research when creating threat models in the power systems domain. Answering the research question, this systematic literature review found six different information sources. These are expert knowledge, logs & alerts, previous research, system's state, vulnerability scoring & databases and vulnerability scanners.

The many different information sources that have been used indicate that there is no standard method that is usually followed. The most common information sources that are used are expert knowledge, previous research, and vulnerability scoring & databases. As discussed in this paper there are many positive and negative aspects with all of the information sources. Because of the availability of information for these sources it might be beneficial to combine all three when creating a threat model in the power systems domain.

References

1. Anwar, Z., Shankesi, R., Campbell, R.H.: Automatic security assessment of critical cyber-infrastructures. In: 2008 IEEE International Conference on Dependable Systems & Networks With FTCS and DCC (DSN). IEEE Computer Society, Los Alamitos, June 2008
2. Beckers, K., Heisel, M., Krautsevich, L., Martinelli, F., Meis, R., Yautsiukhin, A.: Determining the probability of smart grid attacks by combining attack tree and attack graph analysis. In: Cuellar, J. (ed.) SmartGridSec 2014. LNCS, vol. 8448, pp. 30–47. Springer, Cham (2014). https://doi.org/10.1007/978-3-319-10329-7_3
3. Byres, E.J., Franz, M., Miller, D.: The use of attack trees in assessing vulnerabilities in SCADA systems. In: IEEE Conference on International Infrastructure Survivability Workshop (IISW 2004). Institute for Electrical and Electronics Engineers (2004)
4. Chang, Y.H., Jirutitijaroen, P., Ten, C.: A simulation model of cyber threats for energy metering devices in a secondary distribution network. In: 2010 5th International Conference on Critical Infrastructure (CRIS), pp. 1–7, September 2010
5. Chen, T.M., Sanchez-Aarnoutse, J.C., Buford, J.: Petri net modeling of cyber-physical attacks on smart grid. IEEE Trans. Smart Grid 2(4), 741–749 (2011)
6. Chen, Y.T.: Modeling information security threats for smart grid applications by using software engineering and risk management. In: 2018 IEEE International Conference on Smart Energy Grid Engineering (SEGE), pp. 128–132, August 2018
7. Chen, Y.T., Huang, C.C.: Determining information security threats for an IoT-based energy internet by adopting software engineering and risk management approaches. Inventions 4, 53 (2019)

8. Cherdantseva, Y., et al.: A review of cyber security risk assessment methods for SCADA systems. Comput. Secur. **56**, 1–27 (2016)
9. Dai, Q., Shi, L., Ni, Y.: Risk assessment for cyber attacks in feeder automation system. In: 2018 IEEE Power Energy Society General Meeting (PESGM), pp. 1–5, August 2018
10. Dai, Q., Shi, L., Ni, Y.: Risk assessment for cyberattack in active distribution systems considering the role of feeder automation. IEEE Trans. Power Syst. **34**(4), 3230–3240 (2019)
11. Dai, Q., Shi, L., Ni, Y.: A sponsor incentive attack scheme for feeder automation systems. IEEE Trans. Smart Grid **11**, 1440–1452 (2019)
12. Davis, K.R., et al.: A cyber-physical modeling and assessment framework for power grid infrastructures. IEEE Trans. Smart Grid **6**(5), 2464–2475 (2015)
13. Duman, O., Ghafouri, M., Kassouf, M., Atallah, R., Wang, L., Debbabi, M.: Modeling supply chain attacks in IEC 61850 substations. In: 2019 IEEE International Conference on Communications, Control, and Computing Technologies for Smart Grids (SmartGridComm), pp. 1–6, October 2019
14. Eibl, G., et al.: Exploration of the potential of process mining for intrusion detection in smart metering. In: ICISSP, pp. 38–46, January 2017
15. Garcia, L., Zonouz, S.: TMQ: threat model quantification in smart grid critical infrastructures. In: 2014 IEEE International Conference on Smart Grid Communications (SmartGridComm), pp. 584–589, November 2014
16. Grochocki, D., et al.: AMI threats, intrusion detection requirements and deployment recommendations. In: 2012 IEEE Third International Conference on Smart Grid Communications (SmartGridComm), pp. 395–400, November 2012
17. Guan, X., Ma, Y., Hua, Y.: An attack intention recognition method based on evaluation index system of electric power information system. In: 2017 IEEE 2nd Information Technology, Networking, Electronic and Automation Control Conference (ITNEC), pp. 1544–1548, December 2017
18. Hacks, S., Hacks, A., Katsikeas, S., Klaer, B., Lagerström, R.: Creating meta attack language instances using ArchiMate: applied to electric power and energy system cases. In: 2019 IEEE 23rd International Enterprise Distributed Object Computing Conference (EDOC), pp. 88–97, October 2019
19. Han, W., Xiao, Y.: Non-technical loss fraud in advanced metering infrastructure in smart grid. In: Sun, X., Liu, A., Chao, H.-C., Bertino, E. (eds.) ICCCS 2016. LNCS, vol. 10040, pp. 163–172. Springer, Cham (2016). https://doi.org/10.1007/978-3-319-48674-1_15
20. Hawrylak, P.J., Haney, M., Papa, M., Hale, J.: Using hybrid attack graphs to model cyber-physical attacks in the smart grid. In: 2012 5th International Symposium on Resilient Control Systems, pp. 161–164, August 2012
21. Holm, H., Ekstedt, M., Andersson, D.: Empirical analysis of system-level vulnerability metrics through actual attacks. IEEE Trans. Dependable Secure Comput. **9**(6), 825–837 (2012)
22. Holm, H., Sommestad, T., Ekstedt, M., Honeth, N.: Indicators of expert judgement and their significance: an empirical investigation in the area of cyber security. Expert Syst. **31**(4), 299–318 (2014)
23. Jiang, R., Lu, R., Wang, Y., Luo, J., Shen, C., Shen, X.: Energy-theft detection issues for advanced metering infrastructure in smart grid. Tsinghua Sci. Technol. **19**(2), 105–120 (2014)
24. Johnson, P., Lagerström, R., Ekstedt, M., Franke, U.: Can the common vulnerability scoring system be trusted? A Bayesian analysis. IEEE Trans. Dependable Secure Comput. **15**(6), 1002–1015 (2016)

25. Khan, R., McLaughlin, K., Laverty, D., Sezer, S.: Stride-based threat modeling for cyber-physical systems. In: 2017 IEEE PES Innovative Smart Grid Technologies Conference Europe (ISGT-Europe), pp. 1–6, September 2017
26. Lemaire, L., Vossaert, J., De Decker, B., Naessens, V.: Security evaluation of cyber-physical systems using automatically generated attack trees. In: D'Agostino, G., Scala, A. (eds.) Critical Information Infrastructures Security, pp. 225–228. Springer, Cham (2018). https://doi.org/10.1007/978-3-319-99843-5_20
27. Liu, N., Zhang, J., Zhang, H., Liu, W.: Security assessment for communication networks of power control systems using attack graph and MCDM. IEEE Trans. Power Delivery **25**(3), 1492–1500 (2010)
28. Mander, T., Cheung, R., Nabhani, F.: Power system DNP3 data object security using data sets. Comput. Secur. **29**(4), 487–500 (2010)
29. Marksteiner, S., Vallant, H., Nahrgang, K.: Cyber security requirements engineering for low-voltage distribution smart grid architectures using threat modeling. J. Inf. Secur. Appl. **49**, 102389 (2019)
30. McDaniel, P., McLaughlin, S.: Structured security testing in the smart grid. In: 2012 5th International Symposium on Communications, Control and Signal Processing, pp. 1–4, May 2012
31. Nasr, E., Shahrour, I.: Evaluating wireless network vulnerabilities and attack paths in smart grid comprehensive analysis and implementation. In: 2017 Sensors Networks Smart and Emerging Technologies (SENSET), pp. 1–4, September 2017
32. Nazir, S., Patel, S., Patel, D.: Assessing and augmenting SCADA cyber security: a survey of techniques. Comput. Secur. **70**, 436–454 (2017)
33. Patel, S., Zaveri, J.: A risk-assessment model for cyber attacks on information systems. JCP **5**, 352–359 (2010)
34. Paudel, S., Smith, P., Zseby, T.: Attack models for advanced persistent threats in smart grid wide area monitoring. In: Proceedings of the 2nd Workshop on Cyber-Physical Security and Resilience in Smart Grids, CPSR-SG 2017, pp. 61–66. Association for Computing Machinery, New York (2017)
35. Radoglou-Grammatikis, P., Sarigiannidis, P., Giannoulakis, I., Kafetzakis, E., Panaousis, E.: Attacking IEC-60870-5-104 SCADA systems. In: 2019 IEEE World Congress on Services (SERVICES), vol. 2642–939X, pp. 41–46, July 2019
36. Ru, Y., et al.: Risk assessment of cyber attacks in ECPS based on attack tree and AHP. In: 2016 12th International Conference on Natural Computation, Fuzzy Systems and Knowledge Discovery (ICNC-FSKD), pp. 465–470, August 2016
37. Schneier, B.: Attack trees. Dr. Dobb's J. Softw. Tools **24**, 21–29 (1999)
38. Ten, C., Liu, C., Govindarasu, M.: Vulnerability assessment of cybersecurity for SCADA systems using attack trees. In: 2007 IEEE Power Engineering Society General Meeting, pp. 1–8, June 2007
39. Ten, C., Manimaran, G., Liu, C.: Cybersecurity for critical infrastructures: attack and defense modeling. IEEE Trans. Syst. Man Cybern Part A Syst. Hum. **40**(4), 853–865 (2010)
40. Tøndel, I.A., Jaatun, M.G., Line, M.B.: Threat modeling of AMI. In: Hämmerli, B.M., Kalstad Svendsen, N., Lopez, J. (eds.) CRITIS 2012. LNCS, vol. 7722, pp. 264–275. Springer, Heidelberg (2013). https://doi.org/10.1007/978-3-642-41485-5_23
41. Vernotte, A., Välja, M., Korman, M., Björkman, G., Ekstedt, M., Robert, L.: Load balancing of renewable energy: a cyber security analysis. Energy Inform. **1**, 5 (2018). https://doi.org/10.1186/s42162-018-0010-x

42. Wadhawan, Y., Neuman, C.: RL-BAGS: a tool for smart grid risk assessment. In: 2018 International Conference on Smart Grid and Clean Energy Technologies (ICSGCE), pp. 7–14, May 2018
43. Wadhawan, Y., Almajali, A., Neuman, C.: A comprehensive analysis of smart grid systems against cyber-physical attacks. Electronics **7**, 249 (2018)
44. Li, W., Jin, H., You, W.: Attack modeling for electric power information networks. In: 2010 International Conference on Power System Technology, pp. 1–5, October 2010
45. Xiong, W., Lagerström, R.: Threat modeling - a systematic literature review. Comput. Secur. **84**, 53–69 (2019)
46. Yan, J., Govindarasu, M., Liu, C.C., Ni, M., Vaidya, U.: Risk assessment framework for power control systems with PMU-based intrusion response system. J. Mod. Power Syst. Clean Energy **3**(3), 321–331 (2015). https://doi.org/10.1007/s40565-015-0145-8
47. Yeboah-Ofori, A., Islam, S.: Cyber security threat modeling for supply chain organizational environments. Future Internet **11**, 63 (2019)
48. Yu-de, Y., Shuilan, L.: Optimal prevention and control strategy against preconceive faults in electric cyber-physical system. In: 2018 2nd IEEE Conference on Energy Internet and Energy System Integration (EI2), pp. 1–9 (2018)
49. Zhang, B., Li, Q., Zhang, Y., Liu, X., Ni, Z.: Generation of cyber-security reinforcement strategies for smart grid based on the attribute-based attack graph. J. Power Technol. **96**(3), 170–177 (2016)
50. Zhang, H., et al.: A multi-step attack detection model based on alerts of smart grid monitoring system. IEEE Access **8**, 1031–1047 (2020)
51. Zhang, Y., Wang, L., Xiang, Y., Ten, C.: Power system reliability evaluation with SCADA cybersecurity considerations. IEEE Trans. Smart Grid **6**(4), 1707–1721 (2015)
52. Zhang, Y., Xiang, Y., Wang, L.: Power system reliability assessment incorporating cyber attacks against wind farm energy management systems. IEEE Trans. Smart Grid **8**(5), 2343–2357 (2017)
53. Zhang, Y., Xiang, Y., Wang, L.: Reliability analysis of power grids with cyber vulnerability in SCADA system. In: 2014 IEEE PES General Meeting—Conference Exposition, pp. 1–5, July 2014

SSGMT: A Secure Smart Grid Monitoring Technique

Sohini Roy[(✉)]

Arizona State University, Tempe, AZ 85281, USA
sroy39@asu.edu

Abstract. Critical infrastructure systems like power grid require an improved critical information infrastructure (CII) that can not only help in monitoring of the critical entities but also take part in failure analysis and self-healing. Efficient designing of a CII is challenging as each kind of communication technology has its own advantages and disadvantages. Wired networks are highly scalable and secure, but they are neither cost effective nor dynamic in nature. Wireless communication technologies on the other hand are easy to deploy, low cost etc. but they are vulnerable to cyber-attacks. In order to optimize cost, power consumption, dynamic nature, accuracy and scalability a hybrid communication network is designed in this paper where a portion of the communication network is built using wireless sensor networks (WSN) and the rest is a wired network of fiber optic channels. To offer seamless operation of the hybrid communication network and provide security a Secure Smart Grid Monitoring Technique (SSGMT) is also proposed. The performance of the proposed hybrid CII for the generation and transmission system of power grid coupled with the SSGMT during different cyber-attacks is tested using NS2 simulator. The simulation results show that the SSGMT for a joint power communication network of IEEE 118-Bus system performs better than the prevailing wireless CIIs like Lo-ADI and Modified AODV.

Keywords: Critical Information Infrastructure · Wireless sensor network · Cyber-attacks · Remote monitoring · Smart sensor nodes · Smart grid

1 Introduction

An improved and efficient Critical Information Infrastructure (CII) for a Critical Infrastructure System (CIS) gives birth to a smart CIS. It is the incorporation of features like full-duplex communication between the CII entities by the addition of embedded systems, automated metering in the smart homes, power distribution automation, pervasive monitoring etc., that converts a traditional power grid to a smart grid system. It is beyond any question that the CII of a smart grid must be accurate, scalable, and secure enough to instantly identify any kind of abnormal behavior in the entities of the power network, securely communicate that information to the control center and thereby help in taking necessary and timely action to ensure uninterrupted power supply.

As a result, finding the best suited design of a robust CII for smart grid has become a boiling topic of research. In [1] a crude idea of the design of a joint power-communication

© Springer Nature Switzerland AG 2020
A. Rashid and P. Popov (Eds.): CRITIS 2020, LNCS 12332, pp. 59–65, 2020.
https://doi.org/10.1007/978-3-030-58295-1_5

network is given using a test system consisting of 14 buses. Yet, the ground level details of the CII system are missing. The authors of [2], have come up with a realistic design of the CII of a smart grid by taking help from a power utility in the U.S. Southwest; their CII system relies completely on wired channels that either use SONET-over-Ethernet or Ethernet-over-Dense Wavelength Division Multiplexing. However, a completely wired CII is neither cost effective nor energy saving. Every CII entity in [2] draws power and thus a huge amount of power is devoted for monitoring the power network itself. Moreover, isolation of CII entities during a failure or a security threat and addition of a new entity in the network for hardening purpose or fault tolerance is extremely difficult and costly in a wired system.

Smart sensors like Phasor Measurement Units (PMUs) are already gaining popularity in smart grid system for measuring electrical waves. Power generation and transmission, power quality, equipment fitness, load capacity of equipment and load balancing in the grid can also be monitored by data sensing techniques. WSNs are comprised of low powered sensor nodes with easy installation process, lesser maintenance requirement, low installation cost, low power profile, high accuracy and scalability. All these have convinced the researchers that WSNs are a very good choice for the designing of the CII of a smart grid. However, the most common drawback of a sensor node is that it is battery powered and it is not easy to replace its dead battery. As a result, energy conservation becomes important. In the proposed work, energy efficiency is obtained by both energy aware routing technique for Supervisory Control and Data Acquisition (SCADA) data transmission and by the use of more expensive rechargeable Energy Harvesting Relay Nodes (EHRNs) for PMU data transmission to the Control Centers (CC). Also, the nodes and wireless channels are vulnerable to cyber-attacks. Some of the common cyber-attacks in WSNs are discussed in [3].

In this paper, a hybrid CII is designed in which a WSN based communication network is used between a sensing unit placed at a substation like a Remote Terminal Unit (RTU) or a PMU and a regional aggregation point like a Regional Sink node (RS) or Phasor Data Concentrator; and optical fiber based communication is used between the regional aggregation point and the CCs. SSGMT aims at securing the sensed data by means of light weight security protocols used in [4] like Elliptic-Curve-Public-Key Cryptography (ECC), Elliptic-Curve-Diffie-Helman Key exchange scheme (ECDH), Nested Hash Message Authentication Codes (NHMAC) and RC5 symmetric cypher.

The rest of the paper is structured as follows. Section 2 gives an overview of the CII system setup phase for SSGMT. Mitigation of different threats to the proposed network design is discussed in Sect. 3 by adopting a secure routing technique. Section 4 does performance analysis of the proposed scheme SSGMT by means of comparing the simulation results with other existing secure remote monitoring technique for power grid like Lo-ADI [5] and Modified AODV [6]. Sections 5 concludes the paper and discusses the scope for future works.

2   Overview of the CII System Setup Phase for SSGMT

In order to provide a reliable remote monitoring technique for the smart grid, a generic hybrid CII system design is proposed in this section that can be applied on any given power network. In order to illustrate the steps of CII design, the generation and transmission part of a power grid formed by the IEEE 14-Bus system is considered.

Initially, a given power grid is divided into several substations based on [7]. In Fig. 1, the IEEE 14-Bus system is divided into 11 substations. After the substation division, two substations having the highest and second highest connectivity with other substations are selected as Main and backup CCs respectively. As the CCs are selected, all substations are equipped with a router acting as a gateway (GW_i) and a substation server is placed in each CC acting as the access point for the operator. The CC- gateways can receive optical signals from the optical channels and convert them to electrical signals using a photodiode and send those data to server via a wired LAN connection. Other GW_is can receive data from the sensors in that substation via Zigbee and forward that to either the non-rechargeable relay nodes or the EHRNs.

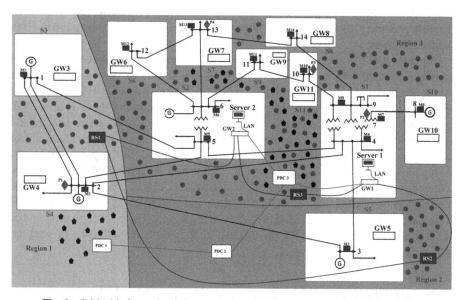

Fig. 1. Critical information infrastructure design for a smart grid of IEEE 14-Bus

The distance between all pairs of substations (S_i & S_j) is calculated as in [2]. Now, starting from a substation S_i with the maximum connectivity among the border substations, all other substations which are within a given distance D of S_i, are marked as substations of a common monitoring region R_x. D is determined on the basis of network size and average distance between substations. Then the next substation which is the closest to S_i but beyond the given distance and which is not yet placed in a monitoring region, is selected and the same process is repeated. This process is continued till every substation is placed within a particular R_x. In Fig. 1, S_1 is selected as the main CC and S_2 is selected as the backup CC. Substations S_3, S_4, S_5 and S_{10} are at the borders of the smart grid area. Among them, S_4 has the maximum connectivity, therefore the region division starts from it and finally, the smart grid network for IEEE 14-Bus system is divided into 3 monitoring regions.

In SSGMT, two different types of Zigbee enabled smart sensors are considered for monitoring the power network entities. The first type is the Measuring Unit (MU) based smart sensors [8] connected to an RTU for measuring SCADA input data and the second type is the Zigbee enabled PMU-based smart sensors or ZPMU [9].

In this step, MU-based sensors (M_i) are placed at every bus but PMU-based sensors (P_i) are placed at some of the buses using an optimal PMU placement algorithm [7]. If there are multiple M_is in a substation then RTU receives the data from all such M_is before forwarding them to the substation gateway (GW_i). Low-cost, non-rechargeable battery enabled relay nodes are randomly dispersed across the network area. These relay nodes can carry the SCADA data to a RS placed at every monitoring region. Each RS is either connected to a neighboring RS or a CC-gateway via optical fiber channels to form a ring structure in order to provide fault tolerance. These RSs now convert the electrical signals obtained from the relay nodes to optical signals using a light emitting diode, associated with each RS. These optical signals are then carried to the CC-gateways via optical fiber channels and other RSs in the ring. TCP based communication is used between the RSs and the CC-gateway.

A phasor data concentrator (PDC), responsible for receiving and accumulating PMU data from multiple PMUs, is also placed at each region of the smart grid and few EHRNs are randomly deployed across the smart grid region. The idea behind the deployment of the two kinds of sensor nodes is that, the cheaper non-rechargeable relay nodes will follow an event-driven hierarchical routing approach to send the SCADA data and the EHRNs will always be active to accumulate synchrophasor data from the substations of each region and send the data to the local PDCs and finally to the CC-gateways. Due to the high volume of PMU data transfer from each substation having a PMU, the sensor nodes carrying them should always be active. IEEE C37.118 standard is maintained for communication of PMU data to the PDCs. PDCs can convert the data to optical signals in the similar way as RSs and send that to the CC-gateways either directly or via other PDCs in neighboring regions. PDCs also use TCP based communication to send the optical data to CCs.

3   Secure Smart Grid Monitoring Technique (SSGMT)

The goal of the CII for a smart grid is to securely transmit the sensed data from the sensors to the CCs and help in remote monitoring of the power grid. In order to achieve this with the help of a hybrid CII, the SSGMT is divided into 3 modules and described in this section.

3.1   Module 1: Data Sensing by Substation Sensors and Forwarding to Substation Gateways

In the first module of SSGMT, the M_i and P_i sensors placed in the substations sense electrical waves from the buses they are placed on and use Zigbee to send the data to the substation gateway GW_i. No security measure is adopted in this step as it is assumed that no cyber attack can harm the communication within a substation.

3.2 Module 2: Data Forwarding by Substation Gateways to RSs and PDCs

The next phase of the hybrid CII system of SSGMT is data forwarding by GW_is. GW_i use two separate methods for forwarding M_i and P_i data. First, the trust values (TV_i) of the non-rechargeable nodes (N_i) and EHRNs are determined by the GW_is of that region by means of forwarding a number of test messages through them to the RSs and PDCs of that region respectively. The TV_i of each node is calculated using Eq. 1.

$$TV_i = \frac{MSG_{delivered}}{MSG_{sent}} * 100 \qquad (1)$$

It is assumed that all the CII entities are provided with a global key GBK which an attacker cannot get hold of even if the entity is compromised. Also, a unique set of elliptic curves is stored in the memory of each CII entity for the purpose of ECC and ECDH protocols [4]. Also, in order to achieve those mechanisms, it is assumed that any pair of entities in the network agrees upon all the domain parameters of the elliptic curves stored in them. Now, rest of module 2 is described using the flowchart below.

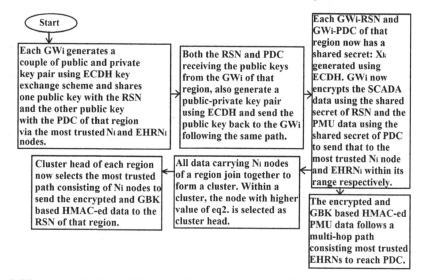

RC5 symmetric cipher [4] is used for the encryption of data using the shared secret. The GBK is used by GW_i to generate a Hashed Message Authentication Code (HMAC) [4] over both the encrypted SCADA and PMU data and attached with the encrypted data for the purpose of authentication of data. Equation 2 is used to select the cluster head. N_i nodes receiving data from GW_i and with highest Candidate Value (CV_i) is selected as the cluster head.

$$CV_i = BP_i * TV_i * Cn_i \qquad (2)$$

In Eq. 2, BP_i represents remaining battery power of N_i, TV_i is the current trust value of N_i and Cn_i is the connectivity of N_i with other nodes in the region. The same path to send data to RSs and PDCs is followed by each GW_i until the RSs or PDCs send a rerouting request to the corresponding GW_i.

3.3 Module 3: Data Forwarding by RSs and PDCs to CC-Gateways

In this module, the RSs and PDCs after obtaining the encrypted and HMAC-ed data from the Ns and EHRNs use the shared secret obtained for that sender GW_i to decrypt the data packets. They also match the HMAC attached with the encrypted data to check if any false data injection took place. In case, the HMAC does not match, the data packet is dropped, and rerouting request is sent back to the sender. The main CC-server use ECC based public key cryptography [4] and generate a public key for encryption and a private key for decryption of data. The ECC based public key of the main CC-server is sent to each of the RSs through the RS-ring and also to the PDCs via other PDCs and the optical channels. The main CC-gateway use a dedicated and secure optical channel to communicate with the backup CC-gateway. This channel is used to share the private key with the backup CC-server. RSs are responsible for data aggregation. Aggregated SCADA data from the Ns are encrypted by the RSs using the public key of the main CC-server. This encrypted data is sent to both the CC-gateways via the RS-ring. In the similar way PDCs send the aggregated and encrypted synchrophasor data via other PDCs to the CC-gateways wherefrom they reach the CC-servers.

4 Simulation Results

In this section, the CII for a smart grid network of IEEE 118-Bus system is considered. The total network region is divided into 8 regions and the power grid is divided into 107 substations. Substation 61 is selected as the main CC and it consists of 3 buses–68,69 and 116. Substation 16, consisting of buses–17 and 30, is selected as the backup CC. In order to analyze the performance of SSGMT in this network setup, a total of 1500 non-rechargeable relay nodes, 500 EHRNs and 8 PDCs are deployed in the network area and NS2.29 is used for simulation. The simulation results are compared with existing WSN based CII systems like Lo-ADI [5] and modified AODV [6] (Figs. 2 and 3).

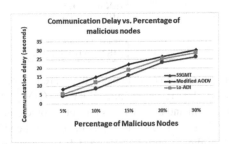

Fig. 2. Communication delay vs. malicious nodes

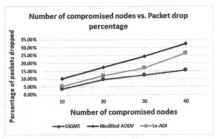

Fig. 3. Number of compromised nodes vs. packet drop

5 Conclusion and Future Works

The region based remote monitoring adopted by SSGMT helps in easy identification of a failure in the power grid or an attack in the communication network of the smart grid.

SSGMT obtains data privacy by the encryption/decryption mechanisms, data integrity and authenticity by the HMACs. Delay, security, power consumption, scalability etc. are optimized by this hybrid network design of SSGMT. Designing a threat model with attacks on smart sensors, gateways or servers and analyzing the effect of cyber-attacks on power grid can be another direction of future work.

References

1. Zhu, W., Milanović, J.V.: Cyber-physical system failure analysis based on Complex Network theory. In: IEEE EUROCON 2017 - 17th International Conference on Smart Technologies, Ohrid, pp. 571–575 (2017)
2. Roy, S., Chandrasekharan, H., Pal, A., Sen, A.: A new model to analyze power and communication system intra-and-inter dependencies. In: IEEE Conference on Technologies for Sustainability (SUSTECH 2020), Santa Ana, pp. 181–188 (2020)
3. Karlof, C., Wagner, D.: Secure routing in wireless sensor networks: attacks and countermeasures. Ad Hoc Netw. 1, 293–315 (2003)
4. Roy, S.: Secure Cluster Based Routing Scheme (SCBRS) for Wireless Sensor Networks. In: 3rd International Symposium on Security in Computing and Communications (SSCC), pp. 368–380, Kochi (2015)
5. Dhunna, G.S., Al-Anbagi, I.: A low power WSNs attack detection and isolation mechanism for critical smart grid applications. IEEE Sens. J. 19(13), 5315–5324 (2019)
6. Sreevidya, B., Rajest, M.: False data injection prevention in wireless sensor networks using node-level trust value computation. In: International Conference on Advances in Computing, Communications and Informatics (ICACCI), Bangalore, India, pp. 2107–2112 (2018)
7. Pal, A., Mishra, C., Vullikanti, A.K.S., Ravi, S.S.: General optimal substation coverage algorithm for phasor measurement unit placement in practical systems. IET Gener. Transm. Distrib. 11(2), 347–353 (2017)
8. Song, E.Y., FitzPatrick, G.J., Lee, K.B.: Smart sensors and standard-based interoperability in smart grids. IEEE Sens. J. 17(23), 7723–7730 (2017)
9. Roy, A., Bera, J., Sarkar, G.: Wireless sensing of substation parameters for remote monitoring and analysis. Ain Shams Eng. J. 6(1), 95–106 (2015)

Networks and IoT

Finding Fast Flux Traffic in DNS Haystack

Williams Surjanto[1]([✉]) and Charles Lim[2]([✉])

[1] Infrastructure Team Indonesia Honeynet Project, Jakarta, Indonesia
wyohanes96@gmail.com
[2] Information Technology Department, Swiss German University,
Tangerang, Banten 15143, Indonesia
charles.lim@sgu.ac.id

Abstract. Fast-Flux (FF), a technique to associate hostname to multiple IP addresses, has been used by cybercriminals to hide their botnet server responsible for its anonymity and resiliency. The operation FF network service, often used for a phishing campaign and propagate malware to attack critical infrastructure, is quite similar to the operation of the Content Delivery Network (CDN) service, making it more challenging differentiating between the two services. In this research, the authors present a case study of how FF operate and can be detected in Internet Service Provider (ISP) network infrastructure, a high volume of DNS traffic was collected over the five months and analyzed by extracting several DNS features and feed into K-means clustering to distinguish between these two services. During the experiment, the authors show that utilizing web service content as one of the elements can differentiate between the two services with a purity value of 0.922.

Keywords: Passive DNS · Fast-Flux · Content Delivery Network · Clustering · Botnet · Malware

1 Introduction

Cybercriminals are always keen to plan unpredictable schemes for spreading their malicious campaign. Domain Name System (DNS) is one of the technologies that is constantly abused by these criminals to redirect internet users to a scamming website that visually look like a legitimate website [1] or used to propagate malware to launch a zero-day attack to critical infrastructure.

To evade detection from ISP and law enforcement, cyber-criminal employs a more robust technique by using Command and Control Server (C&C server) of botnets, with a single domain name associated with multiple IP addresses [2] known as Fast-Flux. Fast-Flux was found in 2007 and used to cover illegal operations such as money laundry and phishing attacks [3,4]. According to Caglayan et al. [5], Fast-Flux botnets have contributed 24% of phishing incidents in 2012 with an estimation of $800 M. Moreover, Fast-Flux commonly used as a host for

© Springer Nature Switzerland AG 2020
A. Rashid and P. Popov (Eds.): CRITIS 2020, LNCS 12332, pp. 69–82, 2020.
https://doi.org/10.1007/978-3-030-58295-1_6

malware distribution; For example, SandiFlux that found in December 2017 used as a proxy for GandCrab ransomware infrastructure concentrated in Romania and Bulgaria [6].

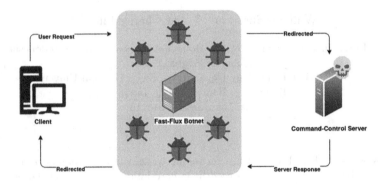

Fig. 1. Fast-Flux mechanism

Figure 1 depicts the mechanism of Fast-Flux used to maintain a phishing website by redirecting requests from the client to the C&C server. Once the C&C server done with the user's request, it then sends back again the response to its botnet, which will redirect it to the user. This mechanism maintains the anonymity and reliability of the C&C server since shutting down service will only affect one of its botnets and can be restored relatively fast by switching to another botnet.

One of the most common techniques to detect these FF botnets is to utilize passive DNS [7], it is introduced by Florian Weimer back in 2005 to fight malware [8]. Passive DNS relies on the idea to capture and collect all of the transaction from the recursive name server on to the centralized database for further analyzing. Figure 2 shows how passive DNS works: it remains between the recursive name server and the destination server (DNS server) to capture all of the outbound and inbound DNS connection. The captured data will be further analyzed using various statistical methods or machine learning. In this research, the author adopted K-means clustering to study FF domains from the captured DNS traffic.

Due to its fast-changing nature of Fast-Flux [9], FF botnets can mimic known services such as Content Delivery Network (CDN)[10]. CDN, also known as dynamic DNS, uses a load balancing technique to keep the infrastructure of the server up and running without concern of downtime. CDN and Fast-Flux have a lot in common, particularly their infrastructure design confusing network administrator.

Amusing enough, in the experiment, the Top Level Domain (TLD) of a legitimate website that uses CDN return web content (i.e. scripts such as HTML, CSS, and JS), whereas response from TLD of FF domains used to host a malicious website return an empty response. This paper proposes a new web service content to distinguish Fast-Flux domains from benign domains and cluster them through correlation.

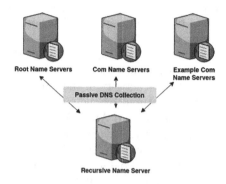

Fig. 2. Passive DNS mechanism

The remainder of this paper is organized as follows. Section 2 describes related research or work of Fast-Flux or botnet detection using passive DNS and clustering. Section 3 presents the research framework, while Sect. 4 discusses implementation setup. Finally, Sect. 5 and Sect. 6 describe the final finding and conclusion respectively.

2   Related Works

There are three ways to collect DNS traffic to detecting Fast-Flux in the network: (i) active DNS probing, (ii) passive DNS probing, and (iii) active service probing [11]. The comparison of the advantages and disadvantages of the three methods is described in Table 1.

Table 1. Comparison of DNS data collection methods

Techniques	Advantages	Disadvantages
Active DNS probing [12–14]	Accurate DNS record Suitable for real time detection	Detectable by botmaster Authoritative name server could stop responding
Passive DNS probing [15–20]	Stealth operation	Less precise not Suitable for real time detection
Active service probing [11]	No control for what is collected Suitable for real time detection	Network congestion may affect results Not scalable for large networks

Perdisci et al. [15] uses passive DNS and opposes active DNS probing, since a high volume of queries to the DNS server may alert botnets owner and block the connection of the user from getting more information about the infrastructure. Thus, passive DNS is preferred to evade detection from botmaster. The collected data is then separated into two features: passive feature, and active feature, and fed into a machine learning model SVM for classification.

In the same way, Antonakakis et al. [16] use passive DNS to detect Fast-Flux through a clustering mechanism called *Notos*. It is used as a reputation engine to find an association of malicious activity in the domains. There are three categories of features that were captured by the engine. The first category is the collection of IP addresses, location, and ASN (Asynchronous System Number). The second category comprises of the average length of domains, the number of distinct TLD, and character frequency. Finally, the last and the third category was the collection of domains contacted by malware from the honeypot. The collected data will be fed into the reputation engine and mapped into the clustering mechanism.

Lombardo et al. [17] proposed *Aramis* framework, which divide into two stages. The first stage starts by filtering known benign domains such as CDN and another popular website to make sure that the dataset is not bloated. The second stage is the metric identification that separated the dataset into two metrics which is static metric to get the DNS features (IP address, Time To Live (TTL), ASN) and history metric collected by observing the changing of DNS features. After the separation, the two metrics will be aggregated into one single anomaly indicator to identify FF domains.

Thomas et al. [19] use hierarchical clustering to arrange DGA (Domain Generation Algorithm) and Fast-Flux into to a particular variant or malware family based on traffic similarity based on Jaccard index.

In contrast, Dietrich et al. [18] use K-means clustering to classify the type of protocol used by a botnet to contact C&C Server DNS, based on predetermined K value. Computationally, K-means clustering will outperform in terms of runtime execution compared to hierarchical clustering, i.e. $O(n)$ vs $O(n^2)$ respectively. Thus for a large dataset, e.g. in an ISP environment, K-means is more suitable [21].

Almomani et al. [20] take a different approach by combining active and passive DNS probing and Adaptive evolving fuzzy neural networks to achieve more accurate detection in Fast-Flux network especially the zero-day attack from the botnet. The framework has detection accuracy to 98% and suitable for a continuous learning system.

Cafuta et al. [22] proposes an FF domain detection algorithm based on two features hard to be changed by botnets. Document fetch delays, that measure the time of response process and analysis of the domain name based on legitimate dictionary words with the assumption that legitimate website used a legitimate word because of digital security policies implemented by the registrar. However, the authors of the research use only dictionary words that come from English, and in order to overcome this limitation, they proposed another new feature according to the number of hits from the search engine.

In this research, to distinguish FF domains from legitimate domains, the proposed framework will use a more stable features that are more difficult to be evaded by botnet. Furthermore, the framework will also not be susceptible to any network delay in the process.

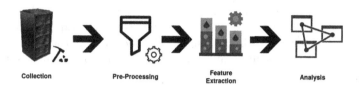

Collection   Pre-Processing   Feature
                                            Extraction   Analysis

Fig. 3. Research framework

3   Research Framework

Figure 3 shows the proposed framework used in this research:

- **Data Collection** - capturing and storing DNS packet. It aims to gather all of the transactions between clients and recursive name servers. To make sure the captured data is not lost, the framework will make a copy of it and stored it into backup storage.
- **Pre-Processing** - filtering relevant data [23] so the framework is not overwhelmed with the captured data.
- **Extraction** - This stage aims to extract the web service content features from the DNS packets (i.e. scripts such as HTML, CSS, Javascript and a combination of these) of the TLD web page.
- **Analysis** - The extracted data will continue to be analyzed for detecting the Fast-Flux domain using K-means clustering to find a correlation of data in groups, defined by parameter K. Following are the K-means clustering process in greater details:

- **Assignment step** - Equation 1 shows how to assigns each data from the nearest centroid. The algorithm starts by choosing a random set of k center-points. Along each update step, all locations of x are assigned to their nearest center-point. If multiple centers have the same distance to the observation, a random one would be chosen.

$$S_i^{(t)} = \left\{ x_p : \left\| x_p - \mu_i^{(t)} \right\|^2 \leq \right.$$
$$\left. \left\| x_p - \mu_j^{(t)} \right\|^2 \forall j, 1 \leq j \leq k \right\} \tag{1}$$

- **Update step** - Equation 2 will reposition the centroid by calculating the mean of the assigned observations to the respective center-points. This will continue until all observations remain at the assigned center-points and therefore the center-points would not be updated anymore. Assignment and update steps will be iterated until one or two of these criteria met: no changing in the cluster coordinate or the maximum number of iterations is satisfied.

$$\mu_i^{(t+1)} = \frac{1}{|S_i^{(t)}|} \sum_{x_j \in S_i^{(t)}} x_j \tag{2}$$

To measure the accuracy of the clustering result, purity [24,25], the external evaluation criterion of cluster quality was chosen. It is considered as a simple and transparent evaluation measure, in which the value provide the percentage of the total number of nodes that were grouped correctly. Equation 3 calculates the purity value, with N = is the number of nodes, k = is the total number of clusters, C(i) is a cluster in C, and t(j) is the classification that has maximum number for cluster C(i).

$$purity = \frac{1}{N} \sum_{i=1}^{k} \max j |c(i) \cap t(j)| \tag{3}$$

To estimate purity value, it needs to compute the confusion matrix (error matrix) by looping through each cluster C(i) and calculate the total of nodes that were classified for each group t(i). Next, pick the maximum value of each cluster, sum it together, and divide by the total nodes from all clusters.

4   Experiment Setup

The following section describes the key components inside the framework which create to detect Fast-Flux using new features and it also includes an explanation of the structure of framework in depth.

Passive DNS is chosen for this research due to its less intrusive nature unlike [12–14]. Farsight Network Message Encapsulation Library (NMSG) [26] is one of the passive DNS tools used to capture the DNS traffic that supports dynamic message types, compression, fragmentation, sequencing, and rate-limiting [27]. Figure 4 presents the system overview inside an ISP network infrastructure, with the traffic that comes from port mirroring through the network switch.

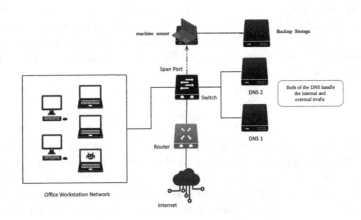

Fig. 4. Passive DNS system overview

To prepare the dataset for the K-means clustering, i.e. web service content and size of the content need to be obtained, a python script is developed to download and store the size of the source code to each of the domain names using urllib2 library. Special python program, running under the sci-kit environment [28], to compute and generate graphs for K-means clustering. In addition, pandas python library is also being utilized for handling complex data structures for statistical computing [29].

5 Results and Discussions

5.1 Data Collection

In this paper, DNS data is collected from October 2018 to March 2019 inside the ISP infrastructure located in Indonesia that serves around 1000 enterprises and 3000 residential users with a total bandwidth of 11 GB+ covering international and local traffic. Figure 5 displays the total DNS records per week in the span of 20 weeks. In the end, the authors collect almost 9 billion raw DNS data with an average of 51 million DNS records each day.

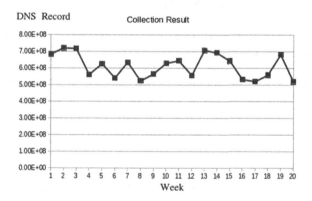

Fig. 5. DNS data size (Weekly)

5.2 Pre-processing Results

To reduce the workload of the framework, DNS dataset will be filtered based on whitelist domains, e.g. legitimate domains from ALEXA top 1 million domain [30], ALEXA top 1 million TLD [31], common domains from Indonesia [32] and the well known CDN services [10] such as Heroku, Akamai and other.

To select the qualified FF domains, the threshold for each of the IP address change rate and the TTL value are compared to some thresholds [15,33]. The threshold for IP address is determined by computing the average value of all unique IP address that map to each of the domain. Furthermore, the domain that changes it's IP address more than the threshold will likely to be the potential Fast-Flux domains. Again, this is due to conventional benign domain tends to have resolve to either one or two IP addresses, whereas, FF domains have multiple IP addresses to maintain high availability for end-user.

The value for TTL has been set to be less than 300 s, based on the dataset collected from during the experiments. FF domains tend to use low TTL value to regularly changing a list of IP addresses for a particular domain name [2]. Any domains that meet those two mentioned criteria will be subject to the next process, i.e. the extraction phase. Figure 6 summarizes 6 (six) major type of domains that are queried by users, and these domains include:

- **Well Known Domain** - contain various popular domains visited by users, such as Google, Facebook, Twitter, and Whatsapp. These domains are excluded from the analysis process.
- **Content Delivery Network (CDN)** - services that provide speed and reliability of legitimate service, e.g. `scontent-sin6-2.cdninstagram.com` and `media-sin6-2.cdn.whatsapp.net` (belongs to Instagram and WhatsApp respectively), Akamai (`www-cdn.icloud.com.akadns.net`), CloudFront, and Cloudflare (`cdnjs.cloudflare.com`) also queried by users.
- **Network Time Protocol (NTP)** - a core service on the Internet to provide accurate time for machines connected to the Internet. In this research, most of the queries go to `cn.pool.ntp.org` and `asia.pool.ntp.org`.
- **Rootserver** - root server domain `a.root-servers.net` mostly queried to obtain certain domain names being queried.
- **Antivirus** - anti-virus domains mostly queried are *.kaspersky-labs.com, *.avast.com and *.mcaffe.com.
- **Advertisement** - domain names that refer to advertising services such as *.googleadservice.com, *.doubleclick.net and *.amazonaws.com

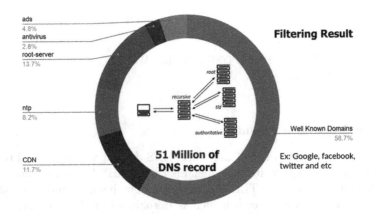

Fig. 6. Filtering result

5.3   Extraction Results

In this phase, the unfiltered domains were queried to obtained both web service content and the size of the domain. Table 2 summarizes the result of the extraction phase, which indicates that malicious domains are found not to respond (i.e. return web content) to the user's queries. This indicates that these two new features could be used to differentiate between a benign vs a FF domain.

Table 2. Extraction result with a new feature

Domain	IP address	WSC*	Type
quiz-api.mentimeter.com.	48	560	Benign
api.amemv.com.	48	1380	Benign
api.appnxt.net.	100	1650	Benign
www.explainjs.com.	48	12000	Benign
re.wikiwiki.jp.	65	1021	Benign
acexedge.com.	49	0	Malicious
reachms.bfmio.com.	99	0	Malicious
ioms.bfmio.com.	99	0	Malicious
ms.cmcm.com.	40	0	Malicious
g.qyz.sx.	50	0	Malicious
kazfv.com.	52	0	Malicious
i1.hdslb.com	32	0	Malicious

*WSC = Web Service Content

We also put to test features used in the previous researches [12–16] using K-means clustering to distinguish FF and CDN domains using K-means clustering as a benchmark whether they can be used to distinguish between benign and FF domain. Following are the features utilized in the tests:

- IP address changed ratio - number of IP network being used by the domain divided by IP address used by the domain in one day
- TTL (Time To Live)
- ASN (Autonomous System Number) - number of unique autonomous system numbers of the domain in a day.
- Network - number of unique IP network used by the domain in a day
- Geolocation - geolocation of each IP address used by the domain in a day
- IP ratio - number of IP network being used by the domain divided by IP address used by the domain in one day
- IP sharing - number of times the IP address intersect with other domain

Table 3 does not show that any significant different values for the tested features for differentiating benign and malicious domains.

5.4   Analysis Result

Figure 7 depicts how web service content can be used as a feature to distinguish between benign domains and FF domains. To determine the optimal value for k, silhouette analysis [34] is used to provide the average distance within the cluster, and with another nearest cluster. The resulted value ranges between −1 and 1, with a value that closer to 1 is the most optimal one. After some calculation, the most optimum value for K turns out to be 3, for K-means clustering, in which the first two clusters, middle and upper clusters (i.e. surrounded by a green box and blue box respectively) contain the benign domains, whereas the lower cluster (i.e. surrounded by the red box) contains FF domains.

Table 3. Extraction Result with common features

Domain	IP address	TTL	ASN	Network	Location	IP ratio	IP sharing
Benign	62	67	2	9	3	6	20
Malicious	69	63	2	11	4	6	13

Table 4 summarizes the results of our experiment over the period of 5 (five) months, distinguishing FF domains from all queried domains, in which the experiments discover 30 to 40 FF domains with the average purity value of 0.922. In addition, there are some false positives on the lower cluster, i.e. mislabeled domains, will be elaborated in the next section.

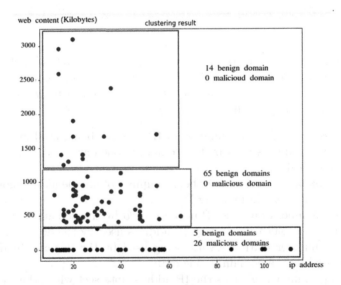

Fig. 7. Clustering result for the first month (Color figure online)

Table 4. Result of detection

Period	Domain			Purity
(month)	Benign	Fast-Flux (FF)	Mislabelled benign	value
1st	84	26	5	0.954
2nd	130	39	15	0.911
3rd	117	35	15	0.901
4th	118	32	13	0.913
5th	110	38	14	0.905
Average				0.922

5.5 Discussions

There are a couple of reasons why web service content can be used as a stable heuristic to detect FF domains:

– Malicious domains including FF domains tend to use a unique path of URL to carry out their instruction or logic, this includes some lexical features such as delimiters('.', '/', '?', '=', '-') and sensitive keywords treat as a parameter ('banking', 'secure', 'signin') to launch their attack in critical infrastructure [35], thus, neglecting the index page where it used the TLD and will not return anything if its queries. Unlike a commercial website built by a legitimate company, the TLD of the domain used to host its official website.
– Malicious domains including FF domains tend to use subdomain in their operation, as Table 4 shows that majority of FF domains used subdomain to host their attack, this approach used to evade blacklist detection by security vendor [36]. However, this leaves the TLD to be unused and when the user tries to get the response it will again return an empty response. Malicious actors tend to evade using TLD as an index to host their attack since it can be easily detected by ISP company in order to make sure their operation covert they more favor to use complex URL path and subdomain.

Moreover, during our experiments, it is also interesting to discover that FF domains reuse the same IP address with the other FF domains, as shown in Fig. 8, in which the diagram shows the many-to-many relationship of these FF domains with their relevant IP addresses [37,38].

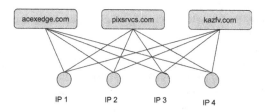

Fig. 8. Fast-Flux domain network

Further analysis on some benign domains identified as FF domains in Fig. 7 reveals that there are 3 domains found to be VPN services located in the USA (shown in Table 5), while the other 2 domains, i.e. `mobi2.hexin.cn` and `re.wikiwiki.jp`, at the time of analysis, are found to be under maintenance leading to redirection that returns an empty response.

Table 5. VPN domain

Domain	IP address	TTL	ASN	Region	WHOIS
cherrychocolate.us	59	18	2	2	Frank nice
sandpile.us	57	29	1	2	Frank nice
carownership.us	56	28	1	1	Frank nice

6 Conclusion

Fast-Flux is a proven technique for cybercriminals to maintain the resiliency of their botnet Command and Control (C&C) Server, by associating hostnames into multiple IP addresses, which belong to machines infected by a botnet. Implementation of Fast-Flux service has a similarity with the Content Delivery Network (CDN) that may lead to false-positive during the threat detection. Using the new web service content feature, our experiments can distinguish Fast-Flux domains from benign domains into clusters adequately with an average purity value of 0.922. For future works, to reduce false-positive further, the research could be extended to include analysis that deals with IP address propagation in the FF network, including a larger set of datasets coming from multiple ISP or higher tier ISP.

References

1. Gupta, B.B., Tewari, A., Jain, A.K., Agrawal, D.P.: Fighting against phishing attacks: state of the art and future challenges. Neural Comput. Appl. **28**(12), 3629–3654 (2017). https://doi.org/10.1007/s00521-016-2275-y
2. Zhou, S.: A survey on fast-flux attacks. Inf. Secur. J. Global Perspect. **24**(4–6), 79–97 (2015)
3. Salusky, W., Danford, R.: Know your enemy: fast-flux service networks. The Honeynet Project, pp. 1–24 (2007)
4. Katz, O., Perets, R., Matzliach, G.: Digging deeper-an in-depth analysis of a fast flux network (2017)
5. Caglayan, A., Toothaker, M., Drapeau, D., Burke, D., Eaton, G.: Behavioral analysis of botnets for threat intelligence. Inf. Syst. E-Bus. Manage. **10**(4), 491–519 (2012). https://doi.org/10.1007/s10257-011-0171-7
6. Proofpoint. Sandiflux: another fast flux infrastructure used in malware distribution emerges (2018). https://www.proofpoint.com/us/threat-insight/post/sandiflux-another-fast-flux-infrastructure-used-malware-distribution-emerges

7. Cantón, D.: Botnet detection through DNS-based approaches (2015). https://www. incibe-cert.es/en/blog/botnet-detection-dns
8. Weimer, F.: Passive DNS replication. In: FIRST Conference on Computer Security Incident, p. 98 (2005)
9. Xu, W., Wang, X., Xie, H.: New trends in fastflux networks (2013). https://media. blackhat.com/us-13/US-13-Xu-New-Trends-in-FastFlux-Networks-WP.pdf
10. Mike Williams, D.A.: The best CDN providers of 2018 to speed up any website (2018). https://www.infoworld.com/article/2994016/network-security/ strengthen-your-network-security-with-passive-dns.html
11. Hsu, F.-H., Wang, C.-S., Hsu, C.-H., Tso, C.-K., Chen, L.-H., Lin, S.-H.: Detect fast-flux domains through response time differences. IEEE J. Sel. Areas Commun. **32**(10), 1947–1956 (2014)
12. Holz, T., Gorecki, C., Rieck, K., Freiling, F.C.: Measuring and detecting fast-flux service networks (2008). https://www.ndss-symposium.org/wp-content/uploads/ 2017/09/Measuring-and-Detecting-Fast-Flux-Service-Networks-paper-Thorsten-Holz.pdf
13. Hu, X., Knysz, M., Shin, K.G.: Measurement and analysis of global IP-usage patterns of fast-flux botnets. In: Proceedings of the IEEE INFOCOM, pp. 2633–2641. IEEE (2011)
14. Koo, T.-M., Chang, H.-C., Chuang, C.-C.: Detecting and analyzing fast-flux service networks. In: Advances in Information Sciences and Service Sciences, vol. 4, no. 10 (2012)
15. Perdisci, R., Corona, I., Dagon, D., Lee, W.: Detecting malicious flux service networks through passive analysis of recursive DNS traces. In: Annual Computer Security Applications Conference, pp. 311–320. IEEE (2009)
16. Antonakakis, M., Perdisci, R., Dagon, D., Lee, W., Feamster, N.: Building a dynamic reputation system for DNS. In: USENIX Security Symposium, pp. 273–290 (2010)
17. Lombardo, P., Saeli, S., Bisio, F., Bernardi, D., Massa, D.: Fast flux service network detection via data mining on passive DNS traffic. In: Chen, L., Manulis, M., Schneider, S. (eds.) ISC 2018. LNCS, vol. 11060, pp. 463–480. Springer, Cham (2018). https://doi.org/10.1007/978-3-319-99136-8_25
18. Dietrich, C.J., Rossow, C., Freiling, F.C., Bos, H., Van Steen, M., Pohlmann, N.: On botnets that use DNS for command and control. In: Seventh European Conference on Computer Network Defense, pp. 9–16. IEEE (2011)
19. Thomas, M., Mohaisen, A.: Kindred domains: detecting and clustering botnet domains using DNS traffic. In: Proceedings of the 23rd International Conference on World Wide Web, pp. 707–712. ACM (2014)
20. Almomani, A.: Fast-flux hunter: a system for filtering online fast-flux botnet. Neural Comput. Appl. **29**(7), 483–493 (2018). https://doi.org/10.1007/s00521-016-2531-1
21. Sonagara, D., Badheka, S.: Comparison of basic clustering algorithms. Int. J. Comput. Sci. Mob. Comput. **3**(10), 58–61 (2014)
22. Cafuta, D., Sruk, V., Dodig, I.: Fast-flux botnet detection based on traffic response and search engines credit worthiness. Tehnički vjesnik **25**(2), 390–400 (2018)
23. Kwon, J., Lee, J., Lee, H., Perrig, A.: PsyBoG: a scalable botnet detection method for large-scale DNS traffic. Comput. Netw. **97**, 48–73 (2016)
24. Manning, C.D., Raghavan, P., Schütze, H.: Introduction to Information Retrieval. Cambridge University Press, Cambridge (2008)
25. Palacio-Niño, J.-O., Berzal, F.: Evaluation metrics for unsupervised learning algorithms. arXiv preprint arXiv:1905.05667 (2019)

26. Biswas, J., Ashutosh, A.: An insight in to network traffic analysis using packet sniffer. Int. J. Comput. Appl. **94**(11), 39–44 (2014)
27. Schiffman, M.: Farsight's network message, volume 1: introduction to NMSG (2015). https://www.farsightsecurity.com/txt-record/2015/01/28/nmsg-intro/
28. Garreta, R., Moncecchi, G.: Learning scikit-learn: Machine Learning in Python. Packt Publishing, Birmingham (2013)
29. McKinney, W.: pandas: a foundational python library for data analysis and statistics. Python High Perform. Sci. Comput. **14**, 1–9 (2011)
30. Umbrella, C.: Alexa one million list domain (2016). http://s3-us-west-1.amazonaws.com/umbrella-static/top-1m.csv.zip
31. Alexa one million list TLD (2016). http://s3-us-west-1.amazonaws.com/umbrella-static/top-1m-TLD.csv.zip
32. Alexa. Top sites in Indonesia - Alexa (2018). https://www.alexa.com/topsites/countries/ID
33. Martinez-Bea, S., Castillo-Perez, S., Garcia-Alfaro, J.: Real-time malicious fast-flux detection using DNS and bot related features. In: 2013 Eleventh Annual Conference on Privacy, Security and Trust, pp. 369–372. IEEE (2013)
34. scikit, selecting the number of clusters with silhouette analysis on kmeans clustering. https://scikit-learn.org/stable/auto-examples/cluster/plot-kmeans-silhouette-analysis.html
35. Patgiri, R., Katari, H., Kumar, R., Sharma, D.: Empirical study on malicious URL detection using machine learning. In: Fahrnberger, G., Gopinathan, S., Parida, L. (eds.) ICDCIT 2019. LNCS, vol. 11319, pp. 380–388. Springer, Cham (2019). https://doi.org/10.1007/978-3-030-05366-6_31
36. Singh, M., Singh, M., Kaur, S.: Issues and challenges in DNS based botnet detection: a survey. Comput. Secur. **86**, 28–52 (2019)
37. Kadir, A.F.A., Othman, R.A.R., Aziz, N.A.: Behavioral analysis and visualization of fast-flux DNS, pp. 250–253. In: European Intelligence and Security Informatics Conference. IEEE (2012)
38. Caglayan, A., Toothaker, M., Drapaeau, D., Burke, D., Eaton, G.: Behavioral patterns of fast flux service networks. In: 2010 43rd Hawaii International Conference on System Sciences, pp. 1–9. IEEE (2010)

A Secure and Privacy-Preserving Data Collection (SPDC) Framework for IoT Applications

Tahani Aljohani$^{(\boxtimes)}$[iD] and Ning Zhang$^{(\boxtimes)}$[iD]

School of Computer Science, University of Manchester, Manchester, UK
tahani.aljohani@postgrad.manchester.ac.uk, ning.zhang-2@manchester.ac.uk

Abstract. Mobile patient monitoring systems monitor and treat chronic diseases by collecting health data from wearable sensors through mobile devices carried out by patients. In the future, these systems may be hosted by a third-party service provider. This would open a number of security and ID privacy issues. One of these issues is the inference attack. This attack allows a single service provider from inferring the patient's identity by collecting a number of contextual information about the patient such as the pattern of interaction with the service provider. Thus a security and ID privacy mechanisms must be deployed. In this paper, we propose a framework called Secure and Privacy-Preserving Data Collection (SPDC) that allows the patient to encrypt the data and then upload the encrypted data on different service providers rather than one while allowing an anonymous linkage for the patient's data which are scattered across different service providers. In this framework, each patient is allowed to select the service providers involved in the data collection, assigns one as the home while the others consider foreign. The patient uses the foreign to upload data while the home is responsible for anonymously collecting the patient's data from multiple foreign service providers and deliver them to the healthcare provider. This framework also shows a novel mechanism to conduct anonymous authentication across different distributed service provides. The framework has been analyzed against the specified design requirements and security threats.

Keywords: ID privacy · Pseudonym · Anonymous authentication · Data authenticity

1 Introduction

The Internet of Things (IoT) can be defined as a network of interconnected objects by means of information and communication technologies to create intelligent systems. One of these systems is the Mobile Patient Monitoring (MPM) system [1,2]. The main function of an MPM system is to provide remote patient health monitoring services anywhere and anytime. A conventional MPM system

© Springer Nature Switzerland AG 2020
A. Rashid and P. Popov (Eds.): CRITIS 2020, LNCS 12332, pp. 83–97, 2020.
https://doi.org/10.1007/978-3-030-58295-1_7

consists of a number of wearable devices worn by a patient, a mobile device carried by the patient, and a backend server owned or managed by a health-care provider. The wearable devices (e.g. wristbands, health patch) are used to measure some health data (e.g. heart rate, blood pressure) from the patient's body, and send the collected data to the remote server via the mobile device. The collected data may be further processed and used for clinical decision making. These collected data are collectively called Patient-Generated Health Data (PGHD) [3,4].

Future MPM systems are anticipated to be built on a third-party service provider owned infrastructures with more resourceful storage and data processing capabilities such as those by Microsoft, Amazon, and Google [5]. When patients' PGHD are handled by a third-party service provider, a number of security and privacy threats arise. These threats include authentication threats (e.g. impersonation), data authenticity threats (e.g modified data), data confidentiality threats, patient ID privacy threats (e.g. inference attack). The UK government has established a regulation called the Data Protection Act [6] to ensure a high level of security and privacy. The DPA regulation has recommended a number of security and privacy requirements including data confidentiality and pseudonymization and anonymization of patient's data. Existing mobile health data collection systems do protect data confidentiality and authenticity [7–12] and and others [10,13–15] combined using pseudonyms to preserve patients' ID privacy. Although this approach would make it more difficult for adversaries to compromise the patients' privacy, this is not sufficient in case the patients are only using one service provider in which some contextual information such as the pattern of communication of each patient (i.e. uploading pattern) is revealed. This information could be used to identify the patient even if the patient is using different pseudonym accounts with the service provider, as proven by [16].

A great deal of research has suggested using the group signature schema and a broadcasting strategy to protect contextual privacy. Boussada et al. [15] present a privacy-preserving aware data transmission protocol that preserves the privacy of a patient's data and the contextual data. To preserve the patient's data privacy, the patient's health data is encrypted and to preserve the contextual privacy (to prevent the inference attack) the protocol used pseudonym IDs combined with a broadcasting strategy. Liang [17] propose a privacy-preserving emergency call scheme, called PEC, enabling patients in life-threatening emergencies to transmit emergency data to the nearby helpers via mobile healthcare social networks (MHSNs). In PEC the ID of the patients is preserved via using group signature. Lin et al. [18] proposed a strong privacy-preserving scheme against global eavesdropping, named SAGE, for eHealth systems. SAGE uses a broadcasting strategy to prevent an adversary from linking patients to their respective physicians. Marin et al. [13] proposed a secure and ID privacy-preserving data collection protocol. The protocol considers a number of security and ID privacy-preserving requirements. To protect the ID privacy of the patient they used a combination of group signature and pseudonym IDs. However, the reliance on a fixed data concentrator for a group of patients would make it easy for that entity to analyze the meta-data associated with the messages and over time cloud build sensitive information about each patient and where they are living.

In this paper, we propose a novel framework called a Secure and Privacy-Preserving Data Collection (SPDC) that allows a patient to upload an encrypted data on different service providers rather than one while preserving the patient's ID privacy. The SPDC architecture consists of multiple service providers and a healthcare provider, the patient has the right to select one service provider as a home service provider (HSP) and others are considered as foreign service providers (FSPs), the home is responsible for collecting the patient's data which are scattered across different foreign service providers and deliver them to the healthcare provider (this is to mitigate the burden of linking of all patients data by one entity which is the healthcare provider). The SPDC framework is a patient-centric in which each patient has the right to generate pseudonym IDs and anonymous credentials called foreign pseudonym certificates (FPCerts) to register with a number of foreign service providers and use their services. However, to register with the home service provider, the healthcare provider issues each patient a certificate called home pseudonym certificate (HPCert). This certificate is used by the patient register with the HSP. After the registration with the HSP, the patient generates a number of FPCerts, one for each FSP. Then the patient requests a blind signature on each certificate from the HSP. The framework has been analyzed in terms of security and privacy requirements.

2 The Design Preliminaries

2.1 SPDC Architecture

The system of the proposed framework consists of three entities: Patients, Service Providers, and a HealthCare Provider. The system model is shown in Fig. 1. The detailed introduction of the entities and their functions are presented as follows: *The patients:* patients are mobile devices. For ease of description, in this paper, we use 'patients' and 'patient' to denote multiple mobile devices and a single device, respectively. Each patient randomly selects a number of service providers (e.g. Google server, Yahoo server, and Amazon server), one of the providers is selected by the patient to be the home service provider (HSP) and the others are considered as foreign service providers (FSPs). To access these FSPs, the patient requests a blind signature from the home on a number of foreign pseudonym certificates (FPCerts) generated by the patient. After getting the blind signature from the home, the patient unblinds the signature and attaches it to the FPCert certificate. Then, uses the certificate to register with the foreign service provider. The home is responsible for anonymously collecting the patient's data which are scattered across multiple foreign service providers and delivering the data to the healthcare provider. Note that, the home is not fixed, one of the patient's foreign service provider will be the home after 24 h. *Service Providers (SPs):* each provider wants to participate in data collection should first register with the healthcare provider. These provides are different and they are geographically distributed across the world. Each service provider can be a home for some patients and at the same time the foreign for other patients. *The Healthcare Provider (HCP):* is the ultimate storage and processing unite of all the patients' data. In addition, it is the certificate authority (CA). The HCP issues a home pseudonym certificate (HPCert) for each patient to be used to register with the home service provider. Note that, the healthcare provider does not know anything about the service providers selected by the patient.

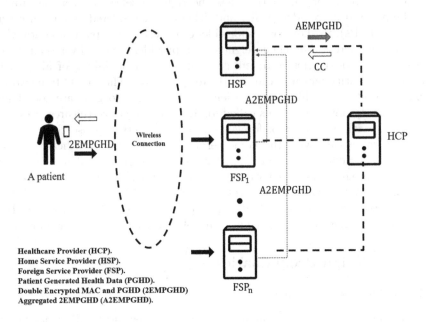

Fig. 1. SPDC architecture.

2.2   Design Requirements

The aim objective of the proposed framework is to provide an efficient secure and ID privacy-preserving which satisfies the following design requirements, where P for identity privacy, S for security, F for functional, E for efficiency.

(P1). Support patient's ID anonymity and unlinkability: Only the healthcare provider should know the real ID of the patient. In addition, different uploading sessions carried out by the same patient can not be linked by unauthorised entity.

(P2). Support anonymous linkability: There are two levels that should be supported. Level (1) each service provider should be able to link each pesudomise request carried out by the same patient. Level (2) the home service provider (HSP) should be able to anonymously link health data of their registered patients from each foreign service provider (FSP).

(P3). The system should be dynamic: This means that the selected home service provider, the selected set of foreign service providers, and the pseudonym IDs for each patient with any service provider should be change every 24 h.

(S1). Support anonymous authentication: Entity authentication ensures that a communicating entity is indeed whom it claims to be without revealing the patient's real ID.

> (S1.1). Support Undetectability: This property means that a patient is able to conceal actions from other parties (service providers and healthcare provider).

(S2). Provide end-to-end data authenticity: Data authenticity assures that data are indeed from the claimed source and that it is exactly the same as what has been sent by the original sender.

(S3). Provide end-to-end data confidentiality: Confidentiality protects data against unauthorized disclosure.

(F1). Support various modes of data collections: These modes includes periodical data collection (e.g. every 5 min) and event-driven data collection.

(F2). Support patient-centric: The patient should has the control to select any service provider, generate pseudonyms and anonymous credentials to access foreign service providers.

(E). Make the design as scalable as possible: The response time on any service provider should not increase sharply as the number of patients and/or the data generated by patients increases.

2.3 Thread Model

There are several security and ID privacy threats. The design of the framework should be protected against them. The threats are as follow.

- Impersonation: is one where an unauthorized entity pretends to be an authorized entity (e.g. a patient, a data collection server) to gain access to a resource and patient privacy information.
- Man in the Middle Attack: is one where an unauthorized entity attempts to intercept communications or messages between the patient and any data collection server.
- Data Forage Attack: is one where an unauthorized entity is able to substitute the patient data with a fake one.
- Data Tampering: is one where an attacker may perform unauthorized modification to the data (e.g., credentials, patient pseudonyms or patient data) being transmitted over the channel.
- Pseudonym Forgery/Theft: is one where an unauthorized entity can generate a valid patient pseudonym, with the intent to deceive a data collection server and misuse the pseudonym to access sensitive patient data.
- Brute Force Attack: is a strategy that involves checking all possible binary combinations of a secret (e.g., a key) until the correct one is found.
- Replay Attack: is one where an unauthorized entity records a transaction message and reuses it later to maliciously do something (e.g. get access to patient data or any other confidential data).

- Repudiation Attack: is one where an unauthorized entity takes a part in transaction, later denies involvement in the transaction.
- Linkability Attacks: is one where an unauthorized entity is able to link multiple uploading or pseudonyms for the same patient.

3   The SPDC Protocol

This section presents the design of SPDC protocol. The protocol consist of two phases, registration with home service provider (HSP), foreign pseudonym certificates (FPCert) construction, and the uploading phase. We assume that, the patient has already registered with the Healthcare provide (HCP) and has obtained the home pseudonym certificate (HPCert) and the home index pseudonym which will be used as pseudonym ID for the patient against the selected home. We also assume that, the patient has selected a number of the service providers and assign one of them as the home while other are foreign. Prior to the detailed protocol description, we first outline the system initialization process. It is worth mentioning that, the underlying cryptography building blocks of the SPDC protocol are asymmetrical encryption (RSA), symmetrical (AES), Elliptic-curve cryptography (ECC), blind signature based on ECC. For the restriction on the length of the paper we will not presents them in this paper.

3.1   System Initialisation

The healthCare provider (HCP) initializes the system by establishing the domain parameters which define the elliptic curve. These parameters are t, a, b, $\mathbb{P}$, and n, where n is the module prime, a and b are coefficients of the elliptic curve equation, $\mathbb{P}$ is the generator point, and t is the number of points in the field. All the entities of the system download these parameters from HCP. Each patient, along with each service providers (SPs), generates an ECC public/private key pair, EPK_i/EPR_i and EPK_{sp}/EPR_{sp}, respectively. The public keys are signed by the HCP and certified in the form of digital certificates. In addition, each SP generates RSA public/private key pairs, RPK_{sp}/RPR_{sp}. The public key is signed by the HCP and certified in a digital certificate. A list of valid service provider certificates is stored in a open-access database. Each entity can access and download them.

3.2   Registration with HSP

During the registration, the patient (P_i) generates a home shared key (HSK_i) using Elliptic-curve Diffie–Hellman protocol. This is done by multiplying the ECC public key of the selected home service provider (EPK_h) with patient's ECC private key (EPR_i), i.e. $HSK_i = EPR_i * EPK_h$. Then it sends the following information to the home service provider (HSP). The information includes the home index pseudonym of the patient (HIP_i), the home pseudonym certificate ($HPCert_i$), and the patient's signature (Sig_i) generated using the private key of the patient on both ($\text{HIP}_i \| \text{HPCert}_i$). The private key is corresponding to the public key which is stated in the home pseudonym certificate (HPCert_i). This step is required only once. However, when the patient changes the home, the process will be repeated again.

$$P_i \rightarrow \text{HSP:}(\text{HIP}_i \| \text{HPCert}_i \| \text{Sig}_i)$$

Upon receipt, the home provider service (HSP) validates the healthcare provider (HCP) signature on the home pseudonym certificate (HPCert_i) and then validates the patient's signature using the ECC public key stated in the certificate. Upon verification, the HSP stores the information in the database entries. Then it sends the following information signed using the home shared key (HSK_i) which is generated using the Elliptic-curve Diffie–Hellman protocol. The information includes, a nonce to be used by the patient to prevent reply attack and a list of tag numbers (e.g. [1–10]) to make the verification of the authenticity of the patient for future request easy for the home. This is done by scooping the search for the verification key within a limited entries in the database (e.g. from 1 to 10). After that, the HSP generates a MAC on the previous information using the home shared key (HSK_i). Finally, it sends the reply message to the patient.

$$\text{HSP} \rightarrow P_i: (\text{tag} \| \text{nonce} \| \text{MAC})$$

Upon receipt, the patient verifies the MAC using the home shared key (HSK_i). It then stores both the nonce and tag. Now, the patient and the HSP is mutual authenticated, the patient can generate foreign pseudonym certificates (FPCerts), one for each foreign service provider. The steps to generates FPCerts are show in the next subsection.

3.3   FPCert Construction

The Foreign Pseudonym Certificate (FPCert) is generated by the patient and blindly signed by the home service provider (HSP). This certificate is used to register with a foreign service provider, one certificate for each provider. Note that, the underlying algorithms (i.e. ECC blind signature) for generating FPCert will not be provided in this paper due to the restriction on the length of the paper. The algorithms are adapted form the work of Wang et al. [19].

The following describes how to generate FPCert certificates. To generate a FPCert certificate the patient first generates the following fields, a temporal elliptic curve key pair ($\text{tPK}_{i,n}$, $\text{tPR}_{i,n}$), a foreign index pseudonym ($\text{FIP}_{i,n}$), where n is the ID of the foreign service provider. The foreign index pseudonym is generated using RSA encryption (Enc). The patient first concatenates the home index pseudonym, the current time (T) and a random value (Rnd) before encrypting them with the home service provider's RSA public key, i.e. $\text{FIP}_{i,n} = \text{Enc}(\text{RPK}_h, \text{HIP}_i \| \text{T} \| \text{Rnd})$. After the generation of both temporal elliptic curve key pair and the foreign index pseudonym, the patient prepares the FPCert certificate. The FPCert certificate consists of the temporal public key ($\text{tPK}_{i,n}$), the foreign index pseudonym ($FIP_{i,n}$), a day-of-expiry (Exp) which is fixed 24 h, and the ID of the patient's home service provider (ID_h). Then, it computes the hash value of the FPCert certificate fields. After that, it blinds the hash value and requests a blind signature on the hash value from the home service provider (HSP). The home generates the blind signature on the hash value using its private key and return it to the patient. Upon receipt, the patient drives the unblind version of signature. Then, it attaches the signature to the FPCert certificate, i.e. $FPCert_{i,n} = \{tPK_{i,n}, FIP_{i,n}, Exp, ID_h, Signature\}$. The patient stores the certificate to be registered later with the foreign service provider.

3.4 Registration with a FSP

The patient sends FPCerts to their respective foreign service providers (FSPs), one for each foreign service provider. The following shows how to register with one foreign service provider. During the registration, the patient (P_i) generates a foreign shared key ($FSK_{i,n}$) using Elliptic-curve Diffie–Hellman protocol. This is done by multiplying the ECC public key of the selected foreign service provider (EPK_n) with patient's temporal ECC private key ($tPR_{i,n}$), i.e. $FSK_{i,n} = tPR_{i,n} * EPK_n$. Then it sends the following information to the foreign service provider (FSP). The information includes the foreign index pseudonym of the patient ($FIP_{i,n}$), the foreign pseudonym certificate ($FPCert_{i,n}$), and the patient's signature (Sig_i) generated using the temporal private key of the patient on both ($FIP_{i,n} \| FPCert_{i,n}$). The temporal private key is corresponding to the temporal public key which is stated in the foreign pseudonym certificate ($FPCert_{i,n}$). This step is required only once in 24 h after that the patient is urged to change this service provider.

$$P_i \rightarrow FSP_n : (FIP_{i,n} \| FPCert_{i,n} \| Sig_i)$$

Upon receipt, the foreign provider service (FSP_n) validates the patient's home service provider (HSP) signature on the foreign pseudonym certificate ($FPCert_{i,n}$) and then validates the patient's signature using the temporal public key stated in the certificate. Upon verification, the FSP_n stores the information in the database entries. Then it sends the following information signed using the foreign shared key ($FSK_{i,n}$) which is generated using the Elliptic-curve Diffie–Hellman protocol. The information includes, a nonce to prevent reply attack and a list of tag numbers (e.g. [1–10]) to make the verification of the authenticity of the patient easy for the FSP by scooping the search for the verification key within a limited entries in the database (e.g. from 1 to 10). After that, the FSP generates a MAC on the previous information using the foreign shared key ($FSK_{i,n}$)). Finally, it sends the reply message to the patient.

$$FSP_n \rightarrow P_i : (tag \| nonce \| MAC)$$

Upon receipt, the patient verifies the MAC using the foreign shared key ($FSK_{i,n}$). It then stores both the nonce and tag. It worth mentioning that the registration process will all the selected foreign service providers should be done offline.

3.5   Uploading Phase

This protocol is executed between the patient and a foreign service provider (FSP). It allows the patient to upload data to the FSP. Then the FSP sends the patient's data to its respective home service provider.

(1) The patient first generates a signed and an encrypted data as follows. It first generates the first MAC on the plain patient generated health data (PGHD) using the shared key (SK_i), this key is known to the patient only and the healthcare provider (HCP), i.e. MAC1 = HMAC(PGHD, SK_i). Then it encrypts both the MAC1 and PGHD using the same key, i.e. EMPGHD = E (SK_i, PGHD $||$MAC1), where E is a symmetrical encryption such as AES. After that, the patient generates the second MAC on EMPGHD using the home shared key (HSK_i), this key is the patient secret key with the home service provider, i.e. MAC2 = HMAC(EMPGHD, HSK_i). Then it encrypts both MAC2 and EMPGHD using the same key, i.e. 2EMPGHD = E (HSK_i, EMPGHD $||$MAC2). This is to facilitate the data auditing (checking the authenticity and integrity of data) by home service provider (HSP) of the patient before outsource data to the healthcare provider (HCP). In addition, prevent both HSP and FSP from learning the content of the patient's data.
(2) Then, the patient generates the fresh pseudonym ($FP_{i,r}$) by first concatenates foreign index pseudonym ($FIP_{i,n}$) with the priority of the data (Pr), and a random number. Then, it encrypts the result with the foreign shared key ($FSK_{i,n}$). The Pr let the FSP know how critical is the patient data without learning the content of the data.

$$FP_{i,r} = E(FSK_{i,n}, FIP_{i,n}||Pr||Rnd)$$

Where E is a symmetrical encryption such as AES. After that, the patient constructs a message (M). This message contains the ID of the foreign service provider (ID_n), the fresh pseudonym of the patient ($FP_{i,r}$), the tag, nonce, and the patient's data ($2EMPGHD_i$), i.e. M = ($ID_n||FP_{i,r}||$tag$||$nonce$||2EMPGHD_i$). Then, the patient generates MAC on the message (M). After that, it sends the uploading request to FSP_n.

$$P_i \rightarrow FSP_n: (ID_n ||FP_{i,r} ||\text{tag} ||2EMPGHD_i ||MAC).$$

The FSP_n receives the request message and performs the following.

(3) The FSP_n verifies the MAC. To verify the MAC, the provider searches for the verification key (i.e. $FSK_{i,n}$) within specific entries in the data base by learning the tag. If the MAC was successful verified, it uses the same key to find the foreign index pseudonym of the patient.
(4) The FSP_n uses the key to recover the patient's foreign index pseudonym by using the reverse operation (AES decryption).
$$FIP_{i,n}||Pr||\text{nonce}||Rnd = D(FSK_{i,n}, FP_{i,r}).$$
(5) After recovering the foreign index pseudonym ($FIP_{i,n}$), the FSP_n validates other parameters including the nonce to protect against a replay attack.

(6) The FSP_n verifies that the FPCert certificate of the patient has not been expired (within 24 h).

(7) The FSP_n checks the priority of the patient's data by looking at the Pr tag, if it is (1) which means urgent, it sends a notification to the home service provider (HSP_i) of the patient.

(8) Otherwise, FSP_n stores the patient's data (i.e. 2EMPGHD) and sends acknowledgement to the patient.

(9) After a period of time, the FSP_n starts aggregating the patient's data ($A2EMPGHD_i$) and then forwards them to the respective home service provider HSP.

$$FSP_n \rightarrow HSP_i:(ID_n||ID_h||FIP_{i,n}||A2EMPGHD_i||MAC).$$

(10) When the HSP receives the message, it first verifies the MAC using the shared key ($SK_{h,n}$), this key is the shared key between the home and the foreign, if the MAC was successfully verified. The HSP recovers the patient's home index pseudonym (i.e. HIP_i), by using the reverse operation (i.e. RSA decryption). This is done as follows. $HIP_i||T||Rnd = Dec(RPR_h, FIP_{i,n})$. Then the home service provider uses the home index pseudonym (HIP_i) to find the home shared key HSK_i to decrypt the patient's data (i.e. 2EMPGHD) and to get the encrypted data of the patient (i.e. EMPGHD) and the associated MAC (MAC1). The home service provider uses the home shared key HSK_i to verify the first MAC. If it successfully verified, it stores the patient's data (EMPGHD) in the database till it being requested by the healthcare provider.

After the patient has received the acknowledgement from the (FSP_n) of the successful storage of the data, the patient has the option to continue uploading on the same provider or break and upload to another service provider.

4 Design Requirements Analysis

Mutual Entity Authentication: This is accomplished by using the home pseudonym certificate (HPCert) and foreign pseudonym certificates (FPCerts). As explained, in the registration phase, mutual authentication between a patient and any service provider is achieved through using a certificate and digital signature. During the uploading phase the patient and the foreign service provider are still mutually authenticated to each other (even though there is no certificate attached to the uploaded message). This is done by generating a MAC signature and attached it to the uploaded message. The MAC is generated using a shared key, which is very difficult for another entity to generate. This is because generating this key involves using both parties' private keys. Obtaining these keys requires computing the elliptical curve discrete logarithm problem (ECDLP), and solving this problem is not easy (S1 is satisfied). In addition, by using digital credentials the healthcare provider is not able to know the home service provider which is selected by the patient. Also through using the blind signature, the home service provider can not know what are the foreign service providers selected by the patient (S1.1 is supported).

Message Authenticity: This is achieved through the sign then encrypt method. As we explained earlier, when the patient uploads his/her PGHD to any foreign provider, the patient needs to sign then encrypt his data twice. This is done by first generating the MAC (MAC1) for plain health data (i.e. PGHD) using a shared key. This shared key is known only to the patient and healthcare provider (HCP). Then, the patient encrypts both MAC1 and the PGHD using the same shared key. The result is the EMPGHD. Then, the patient generates the second MAC (MAC2) for EMPGHD. Then encrypts both MAC2 and EMPGHD using a Home Shared key (HSK) known only to the patient and his/her home service provider (HSP). The result is the 2EMPGHD. Therefore, when the HSP receives the patient's 2EMPGHD from different foreign providers, the HSP verifies the MAC2 associated with each EMPGHD. The same is applied with the HCP which verifies the authenticity and integrity of the data by verifying MAC1 associated with PGHD (S2 is satisfied).

Message Confidentiality: The patient's data are protected by the encryption process. To allow a foreign service provider to learn if the patient's health condition is urgent, the framework allows the patient to encapsulate the priority of health data (PR) within each fresh pseudonym (S3 is satisfied).

Patient's ID Anonymity and Unlinkability: A patient's real ID is known only to the authorised entity (i.e. healthcare provider). The patient's home and foreign servers know the patient's home and foreign index pseudonyms respectively. For each uploading to any foreign service provider, the patient uses a fresh pseudonym to prevent linking multiple uploading sessions by unauthorized entity (P1 is satisfied).

Anonymous Linkability: Level (1) of anonymous linkability is achieved by allowing each home service provider (HSP) to link their patients' data to their respective home index pseudonyms. Level (2) is achieved by allowing each foreign service provider (FSP) to link each fresh pseudonym carried out by the same patient to the patient's foreign index pseudonyms (P2 is satisfied).

Various Modes of Collection: The periodic and event-driven modes are supported. To distinguish an urgent data from normal data we are using the priority tag. For an urgent case, the priority tag is (1) and for a normal case, it is (0). This functional requirement is achieved with the alignment of security requirements. The priority tag is encoded in each uploading pseudonym (F1 is satisfied).

Patient Centric: This is achieved as follows. First, allow the patient to select a number of service providers then assign one as the home service provider while the others as foreign service providers. Second, the patient generates the foreign index pseudonyms and the FPCert certificates which are used to register with the foreign providers. Third, the patient can generate a fresh pseudonyms for each uploading (F2 is satisfied).

Scalable: This is achieved by allowing multiple service provider to collect and anonymously link patients' data (E is satisfied).

5 Security Analysis

In this section the SPDC is analyzed against the threats that are identified in Sect. 2.3. Alice is an authorize patient. Eve is an adversary.

Theorem 1. *SPDC is protected against impersonation attack.*

Proof. Suppose that Eve learns Alice's certificate (i.e. HCert/FCert). Eve is trying to play Alice's role and deceive a service provider (SP). Eve sends the certificate to the SP. The SP accepts the certificate from Eve and asks her to prove the knowledge of the private key which is corresponding to the public key stated in the certificate. Eve needs to generate a digital signature using the private key. Eve fails to generate the digital signature as she does not has the private key. Fortunately, Eve fails to impersonate Alice.

Theorem 2. *SPDC is protected against data forgery attack.*

Proof. Suppose an FSP tries to forge Alice's data by adding a fake PGHD for the sake of getting high incentives as a result of storing more data for Alice. Fortunately, the FSP will not be able to generate fake PGHD for Alice. This is because the FSP needs to obtain two keys, the shared key (SK) with the healthcare provider to generate EMPGHD and the home shared key (HSK) with Alice's HSP to generate 2EMPGHD.

Theorem 3. *SPDC is protected against pseudonym forgery attack.*

Proof. Suppose Eve wants to generate Alice's fresh pseudonym. As we explained previously to generate a fresh pseudonym, Eve needs to know the foreign shared key (FSK). This key is hard to obtain. This is because the generation of this key involves the knowledge of Alice's private key. The knowledge of the private key lies in solving the elliptic curve discrete logarithm problem (ECDLP) which has been proven through years it is computationally infeasible.

Theorem 4. *SPDC is protected against replay attack.*

Proof. Suppose Eve tries to replay one uploading message to disturb an FSP and make it store duplicated data for Alice. Eve forwards old uploading messages to the FSP. After the FSP performed all verifications, it verifies the freshens of the nonce. The FSP discovers that the messages sent by Eve are old. The FSP discards the messages.

Theorem 5. *SPDC is protected against man in the middle attack.*

Proof. Suppose Eve tries to intercept messages that are passed back and forth between Alice and a service provider to steal the shared key, substitutes its own, and makes it appear to Alice that it is the server, and to the server that it is Alice. Fortunately, the secret key between Alice and any SP is generated without exchanging any private keys by using Diffie–Hellman key exchange protocol. In addition, suppose Eve tries to eavesdrop messages between Alice and the SP, Eve will not be able to gain any valuable information as Alice's data is encrypted even Alice's current health status (i.e. urgent or normal) is encapsulated within the fresh pseudonym.

Theorem 6. *SPDC is protected against brute force attack.*

Proof. Suppose Eve wants to work out Alice's real ID from her fresh pseudonym. Using a brute force attack method, Eve would need to guess three symmetric keys and one asymmetrical key which requires $2^{128} * 2^{128} * 2^{2048} * 2^{128}$ attempts (more than $1.02 * 10^{18}$ years of tries).

Theorem 7. *SPDC is protected against reputation attack.*

Proof. Messages which are exchanged between Alice and a service provider contain digital signatures. The signature is generated using Alice's private key or by a shared key. These keys are very hard to obtain as we explained earlier.

Theorem 8. *SPDC is protected against inference Attack.*

Proof. As we know a patient has different index pseudonyms one for each service provider. These index pseudonyms are not fixed. The patient has the right to change the service providers and the corresponding index pseudonyms every day. In addition, for each request with the same SP, the patient is using fresh pseudonyms generated based on the corresponding index pseudonyms. Linking multiple index pseudonyms and multiple fresh pseudonyms to the same patient is a challenging task.

6 Conclusion

To protect the security and ID privacy of patients in MHM systems we designed a secure anonymous data collection framework called SPDC. Our proposed framework has advantages of using multiple service providers to collect a patient's data to prevent a single provider from inferring the patient's identity based on the pattern of interactions, allow the patient to generate pseudonym identities and certificates to access these service providers, and allow each patient's home service provider for anonymously linking the patient's data which are scattered across different foreign service providers. Then, the home service provider of the patient delivers the patient's data after aggregation to the healthcare provider. The requirements analysis of the framework is conducted to ensure the ID privacy-preserving, mutual anonymous authentication, data authenticity and confidentiality, patient-centric, and scalability.

References

1. Al-Fuqaha, A., Guizani, M., Mohammadi, M., Aledhari, M., Ayyash, M.: Internet of things: a survey on enabling technologies, protocols, and applications. IEEE Commun. Surv. Tutor. **17**(4), 2347–2376 (2015)
2. Islam, S.R., Kwak, D., Kabir, M.H., Hossain, M., Kwak, K.-S.: The internet of things for health care: a comprehensive survey. IEEE Access **3**, 678–708 (2015)

3. Paliwal, G., Kiwelekar, A.W.: A comparison of mobile patient monitoring systems. In: Huang, G., Liu, X., He, J., Klawonn, F., Yao, G. (eds.) HIS 2013. LNCS, vol. 7798, pp. 198–209. Springer, Heidelberg (2013). https://doi.org/10.1007/978-3-642-37899-7_17

4. Pawar, P., Jones, V., Van Beijnum, B.-J.F., Hermens, H.: A framework for the comparison of mobile patient monitoring systems. J. Biomed. Inform. **45**(3), 544–556 (2012)

5. Microsoft reporter: The NHS is about to take an 'important' step into the cloud, says microsoft, January 2018. https://news.microsoft.com/en-gb/2018/01/19/the-nhs-is-about-to-take-an-important-step-into-the-cloud-says-microsoft/

6. Kemp, R.: Legal aspects of cloud security. Comput. Law Secur. Rev. **34**(4), 928–932 (2018)

7. Chen, M., Qian, Y., Chen, J., Hwang, K., Mao, S., Hu, L.: Privacy protection and intrusion avoidance for cloudlet-based medical data sharing. IEEE Trans. Cloud Comput. (2016)

8. Lounis, A., Hadjidj, A., Bouabdallah, A., Challal, Y.: Secure and scalable cloud-based architecture for e-health wireless sensor networks. In: 2012 21st International Conference on Computer Communications and Networks (ICCCN), pp. 1–7. IEEE (2012)

9. Layouni, M., Verslype, K., Sandıkkaya, M.T., De Decker, B., Vangheluwe, H.: Privacy-preserving telemonitoring for eHealth. In: Gudes, E., Vaidya, J. (eds.) DBSec 2009. LNCS, vol. 5645, pp. 95–110. Springer, Heidelberg (2009). https://doi.org/10.1007/978-3-642-03007-9_7

10. Mtonga, K., Yang, H., Yoon, E.-J., Kim, H.: Identity-based privacy preservation framework over u-healthcare system. In: Park, J.J.J.H., Ng, J.K.-Y., Jeong, H.Y., Waluyo, B. (eds.) Multimedia and Ubiquitous Engineering. LNEE, vol. 240, pp. 203–210. Springer, Dordrecht (2013). https://doi.org/10.1007/978-94-007-6738-6_26

11. Gope, P., Hwang, T.: BSN-care: a secure IoT-based modern healthcare system using body sensor network. IEEE Sens. **16**(5), 1368–1376 (2016)

12. Simplicio, M.A., Iwaya, L.H., Barros, B.M., Carvalho, T.C., Näslund, M.: SecourHealth: a delay-tolerant security framework for mobile health data collection. IEEE J. Biomed. Health Inform. **19**(2), 761–772 (2014)

13. Marin, E., Mustafa, M.A., Singelée, D., Preneel, B.: A privacy-preserving remote healthcare system offering end-to-end security. In: Mitton, N., Loscri, V., Mouradian, A. (eds.) ADHOC-NOW 2016. LNCS, vol. 9724, pp. 237–250. Springer, Cham (2016). https://doi.org/10.1007/978-3-319-40509-4_17

14. Wang, G., Lu, R., Guan, Y.L.: Achieve privacy-preserving priority classification on patient health data in remote eHealthcare system. IEEE Access **7**, 33 565–33 576 (2019)

15. Boussada, R., Hamdane, B., Elhdhili, M.E., Saidane, L.A.: Privacy-preserving aware data transmission for IoT-based e-health. Comput. Netw. **162**, 106866 (2019)

16. Perez, B., Musolesi, M., Stringhini, G.: You are your metadata: identification and obfuscation of social media users using metadata information. In: Twelfth International AAAI Conference on Web and Social Media (2018)

17. Liang, X., Lu, R., Chen, L., Lin, X., Shen, X.: PEC: a privacy-preserving emergency call scheme for mobile healthcare social networks. J. Commun. Netw. **13**(2), 102–112 (2011)

18. Lin, X., Lu, R., Shen, X., Nemoto, Y., Kato, N.: SAGE: a strong privacy-preserving scheme against global eavesdropping for eHealth systems. IEEE J. Sel. Areas Commun. **27**(4), 365–378 (2009)
19. Wang, C.-H., Liao, M.-Z.: Security analysis and enhanced construction on ECDLP-based proxy blind signature scheme. Int. J. E-Educ. E-Bus. E-Manag. E-Learn. **4**(1), 47 (2014)

Correction to: A Systematic Literature Review of Information Sources for Threat Modeling in the Power Systems Domain

Engla Ling, Robert Lagerström, and Mathias Ekstedt

Correction to:
Chapter "A Systematic Literature Review of Information Sources for Threat Modeling in the Power Systems Domain" in: A. Rashid and P. Popov (Eds.): *Critical Information Infrastructures Security*, LNCS 12332, https://doi.org/10.1007/978-3-030-58295-1_4

Chapter 4, "A Systematic Literature Review of Information Sources for Threat Modeling in the Power Systems Domain" was previously published non-open access. It has now been changed to open access under a CC BY 4.0 license and the copyright holder updated to 'The Author(s)'. The book has also been updated with this change.

The updated version of this chapter can be found at
https://doi.org/10.1007/978-3-030-58295-1_4

A. Rashid and P. Popov (Eds.): CRITIS 2020, LNCS 12332, p. C1, 2021.
https://doi.org/10.1007/978-3-030-58295-1_8

Author Index

Printed in the United States
by Baker & Taylor Publisher Services